Royal Surrey
NHS Foundation Trust

Library & Knowledge Services

Education Centre
Royal Surrey NHS Foundation Trust
Egerton Road
Guildford
GU2 7XX

www.libraryroyalsurrey.nhs.uk

Tel: 01483 464137 (ex 4247)

Email: rsc-tr.library@nhs.net

WORLD CLASS CARE
FOR OUR COMMUNITY

Burnout and Trauma Related Employment Stress

Melissa L. Holland • Stephen E. Brock
Taylor Oren • Maciel van Eckhardt

Burnout and Trauma Related Employment Stress

Acceptance and Commitment Strategies in the Helping Professions

 Springer

Melissa L. Holland
California State University, Sacramento
Sacramento, CA, USA

Taylor Oren
California State University, Sacramento
Sacramento, CA, USA

Stephen E. Brock
California State University, Sacramento
Sacramento, CA, USA

Maciel van Eckhardt
California State University, Sacramento
Sacramento, CA, USA

ISBN 978-3-030-83491-3   ISBN 978-3-030-83492-0   (eBook)
https://doi.org/10.1007/978-3-030-83492-0

This Springer imprint is published by the registered company Springer Nature Switzerland AG
The registered company address is: Gewerbestrasse 11, 6330 Cham, Switzerland

I dedicate this book to all those in the helping professions; to my children, Sophia and Colette; and to my mentor, the late Kenneth Merrell, who gave me my start on how to teach, research, mentor, and be a lifelong learner.

-Melissa L. Holland

To my colleagues, who from their work providing school mental health crisis interventions have found the burden of secondary traumatic stress a heavy load. You are all very brave, knowing what you know about this reality, yet still agreeing to help our nation's school children cope with school-associated crises.

-Stephen E. Brock

To the unsung heroes of our society—the helpers, educators, parents, and people who bravely choose empathy even when their cups are close to empty. May you be filled up and feel the meaningfulness of your work.

-Taylor Oren

For my co-authors, my family and partner, and to the devoted individuals who work earnestly to help and support others.

-Maciel van Eckhardt

Preface

Caregiving can take a heavy toll on mental wellbeing. As a consequence of providing care to clients (or family members), particularly those who have had traumatic experiences, all caregivers and professionals are at risk for burnout and trauma-related employment stress (TRES) conditions (also referred to as compassion fatigue, secondary traumatic stress, and vicarious trauma). The need to assertively address this challenge has never been more relevant as the prevalence of increased trauma and stressful work experiences related to the COVID-19 pandemic appears to have played a role in elevating the risk for post-traumatic stress disorder symptoms among public health workers (Bryant-Genevier et al., 2021). When providers are suffering from conditions related to burnout and TRES, there can be profound physical, psychological, and organizational consequences. In addition to affecting the professional, these employment-related injuries can negatively affect the clients that the helper has dedicated themselves to serve. From the review of the literature, which we summarize in this book, we have found that TRES includes commonalities across helping disciplines, including presenting symptoms and preventative factors.

This book is aimed at how to intervene in and prevent burnout and TRES in the helping professionals. As a vehicle for intervention, the theory of, and tools embedded in, Acceptance and Commitment Therapy (ACT) is highlighted. The goal of ACT is not to eliminate certain parts of our experience, but rather to learn how to experience life more fully, without as much struggle and with vitality and commitment. Further, the goal of ACT includes the reduction of suffering via increasing our psychological flexibility, thereby allowing us to engage in committed action toward our valued personal and professional goals.

We hope you find this book useful, whether you yourself are in need of support or are a provider helping others who are suffering from burnout or TRES conditions. Within the pages of this volume, we hope to emphasize that burnout and TRES are both preventable and treatable. We anticipate that this book will help you address the challenge of burnout and TRES and have both greater personal wellbeing and a continued ability to take care of those you serve.

Sacramento, CA, USA

Melissa L. Holland
Stephen E. Brock
Taylor Oren
Maciel van Eckhardt

Reference

Bryant-Genevier, J., Rao C.Y., Lopes-Cardozo B, Kone, A., Rose, C., Thomas, I., Orquiola, D., Lynfield, R., Shah, D., Freeman, L., Becker, S., Williams, A., Gould, D. W., Tiesman, H., Lloyd, G., Hill, L. Byrkit, R. (2021). Symptoms of depression, anxiety, post-traumatic stress disorder, and suicidal ideation among state, tribal, local, and territorial public health workers during the COVID-19 pandemic – United States, March-April 2021. *Morbidity and Mortality Weekly Report.* Advanced online publication. https://doi.org/10.15585/mmwr.mm7026e1externalicon.

Acknowledgments

We would like to acknowledge all those in the helping professions, including but not limited to, the students in our School Psychology Program at Sacramento State University and the countless providers in the educational, psychological, veterinary, and medical fields whom we have interviewed, worked with, and served over the last several years as we have compiled the information included in this book. A special thank you to Sheila Stein, who assisted with editing, and Sophia Beckette, our illustrator for this book.

-Melissa Holland, PhD
-Stephen E. Brock, PhD, NCSP, LEP
-Taylor N. Oren, EdS, APCC
-Maciel van Eckhardt, EdS, APCC
California State University, Sacramento

Contents

About the Authors

Melissa L. Holland, PhD, is Professor of School Psychology at the California State University, Sacramento (CSUS), and has a private practice specializing in work with children, adolescents, and adults. She is both a licensed clinical psychologist and a certified school psychologist. Dr. Holland has researched and published extensively in the area of mental health on various topics, including emotional and behavioral problems in children, mindfulness interventions, telehealth services, and trauma and homelessness. She also presents workshops at regional and national conferences on the topic of mental health and acts as a consultant in schools and in the medical field, including veterinary settings, focused on burnout and trauma-informed practices.

Stephen E. Brock, PhD, NCSP, LEP, is Professor and the School Psychology Program Coordinator at California State University, Sacramento (CSUS). He is a nationally certified school psychologist and licensed educational psychologist, who worked for 18 years as a school psychologist in California before joining the CSUS faculty. Dr. Brock is a past president of the National Association of School Psychologists and has researched and published extensively in the area of mental health crisis interventions. He also presents workshops at regional, national, and international conferences on the topic of mental health and acts as a consultant to schools around the world.

Taylor Oren, EdS, APCC, is trained in school psychology and clinical psychology. She has worked in a variety of educational and community-based settings, including foster care, hospital and substance abuse treatment, homeless rehabilitation, and primary and secondary schools. Her research has included the impact of trauma among homeless youth populations with implications for increased social-emotional learning opportunities. Ms. Oren also presents at local, state, and national conferences on secondary traumatic stress in the school setting and focuses on individual and systems-level prevention and intervention.

Maciel van Eckhardt, EdS, APCC, is a school psychologist in the East Bay Area in California. She previously worked in a community program for adults and youth with developmental disabilities, applied behavior analysis in-home therapy for youth who have autism spectrum disorder, within primary and secondary schools, and in a homeless rehabilitation program for women and children. Ms. van Eckhardt presents at local, state, and national presentations on the topic of secondary traumatic stress among school staff and related interventions. Her research has included the behavioral and mental health impacts of trauma among youth experiencing homelessness. Ms. van Eckhardt's research interests include school climate, equitable practices, universal supports, trauma-informed practices, and systems-level interventions.

Chapter 1
Introduction to Burnout and Trauma-Related Employment Stress

As a professional consequence of listening and striving to understand clients' traumatic circumstances, a variety of professionals are at risk for burnout and trauma-related employment stress (TRES) conditions. In the words of van der Merwe and Hunt (2019), as professionals empathize with clients, their minds can be flooded with traumatic images resulting "in a diminishing of their capacity to contain, and not collapse under, the weight of another's trauma" (p. 16). This chapter serves as an introduction to these job stress injuries and the concepts of *burnout*, *vicarious trauma*, *secondary traumatic stress*, and *compassion fatigue*. It begins with our attempt to define these constructs and report their risk factors. Next, it examines the prevalence of these challenges within various disciplines and then explores their physical, psychological, and organizational consequences. Finally, the purpose of this book is overviewed, focusing on the technique of acceptance and commitment therapy (ACT) as an intervention for burnout and TRES.

Definitions

Burnout, vicarious trauma, secondary traumatic stress, and compassion fatigue are separate but related constructs and each has significant negative consequences for individuals and organizations (Cieslak et al., 2014). Initially, these terms were coined to better understand the sometimes toxic consequences of human service employment. However, for the purposes of this book, we are applying it to any professional caregiver (e.g., we would include the work of veterinarians as having the potential to generate these stress-related injuries).

As illustrated in Fig. 1.1, each of these challenges has their origins in work-related stress. These stressors can be chronic more general work-related stress, or they can be more specifically associated with work-related empathy-based

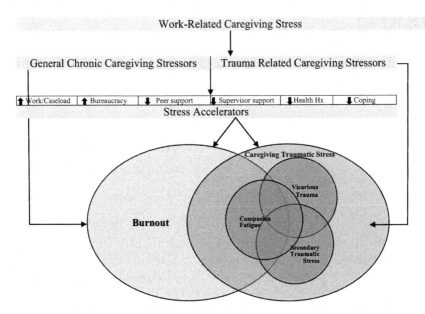

Fig. 1.1 Relationships among burnout, vicarious trauma, secondary traumatic stress, and compassion fatigue

exposure to the traumatic stressors of clients (Newell & MacNeil, 2010; Rauvola et al., 2019). While the former is associated with the phenomena known as professional burnout, the latter has been associated with the terms vicarious trauma, secondary traumatic stress, and compassion fatigue (each of which, as illustrated in Fig. 1.1, has been suggested to overlap with and to be considered a form of burnout). Cieslak et al. (2014) have suggested that burnout and TRES may share as much as 48% of symptom variance, and that compassion fatigue appears to have a stronger relationship with burnout.

Common to all of these constructs is the fact that they are associated with and can be exacerbated by both organizational and individual factors that can increase stress levels. These stress accelerators include high caseloads (especially with traumatized clients), a challenging bureaucracy (especially when it is viewed as unfair and inflexible), a lack of peer support (especially prolonged interpersonal stress), a lack of supervision and support (especially when the impact of work stress is not acknowledged), poor health (especially mental illness and prior traumatic stress), and ineffective or maladaptive coping (Barak et al., 2001; Lerias & Byrne, 2003; Lloyd et al., 2002; Maslach & Leiter, 2016; Newell & MacNeil, 2010; Rupert et al., 2015; Vlăduţ & Kállay, 2010; Yang & Hayes, 2020). Next, we offer a more complete discussion of how these separate but related terms are defined.

Burnout

First recognized within the clinical literature in the mid-1970s (Perlman & Hartman, 1982), burnout has only recently made its way into a diagnostic classification system (Kirsch, 2019). As defined within the 11th revision of the International Classification of Diseases (ICD-11; World Health Organization [WHO], 2019), burnout is considered an occupational phenomenon (not to be used to "describe experiences in other areas of life" para. 1). While not suggested to be a medical condition per se, it is offered within ICD-11 as a factor that can influence health status. Although burnout is typically considered a job-related and situation-specific syndrome, recent study has suggested that burnout and more pervasive depression are related (but separate) to psychological syndromes (Maslach & Leiter, 2016). The American Psychiatric Association (APA, 2013) reports that burnout's "relationship to depression, suicidality and other psychiatric conditions is under study" (p. 3). That said, IDC-11 identifies "exclusions" for burnout to include (a) adjustment disorder, (b) disorders specifically associated with stress, (c) anxiety or fear-related disorders, and (d) mood disorders. Most recent efforts to define burnout have included the dimensions of (a) exhaustion, (b) cynicism, and (c) inefficacy (e.g., APA, 2013; Maslach & Leiter, 2016; Montero-Marín et al., 2011; Newell & MacNeil, 2010; WHO, 2019). According to Montero-Marín et al. (2016), "Exhaustion is the feeling of not being able to offer any more of oneself at work; cynicism represents a distant attitude towards work, those served by it and colleagues; inefficacy is the feeling of not performing tasks adequately" (p. 2). Each of these aspects of burnout is suggested to develop as a result of ineffective coping with job-related stress.

Regarding factors that contribute to burnout, Rupert et al.'s (2015) review of the literature identifies work demands, employment resources, personal resources, and home life factors as all playing a role in professional burnout. Work demands that increase burnout risk include greater number of hours worked and greater number of hours engaged in administrative or paperwork activities. The nature of clients served also affected burnout, with having clients who are threatening or suicidal, who test limits, and who are psychotic all increasing risk; over-involvement with clients also increased risk.

Employment resources associated with risk include a degree of perceived control over work demands, with professionals who view themselves as having little control over work having a greater risk of burnout. Supervisor and peer support were found to be associated with burnout, with those feeling more supported at work having lower risk (Rupert et al., 2015).

Personal resources associated with burnout included coping and self-care strategies. In terms of coping strategies, avoidance (e.g., sleeping more, substance abuse, and wishing the job problems would end) or emotion focus (e.g., alcohol, venting, and denial) coping increased risk. Conversely, problem-focused coping (e.g., seeking support, planning) decreased risk for some aspects of burnout. Regarding self-care, professionals who maintained a sense of control, acknowledged positive work experiences, balanced work and personal life, and monitored themselves experienced less burnout. Finally, home-life activities associated with reduced risk for professional burnout included having good work-life balance, recreational opportunities, and social support (Rupert et al., 2015).

Trauma-Related Employment Stress

Overlapping with, yet considered distinct from, professional burnout is several types of TRES. These include vicarious trauma (VT), secondary traumatic stress (STS), and compassion fatigue (CF). Frequently, these are used as interrelated terms (Day & Anderson, 2011; Newell & MacNeil, 2010), and they do have much in common. Specifically, they may be experienced by any caregiving professional, are a consequence of empathetic engagement with clients' trauma narratives, and (like burnout) affect the ability to perform professional responsibilities (Nimmo & Huggard, 2013). However, from our review of the literature, we do believe there are some meaningful distinctions to be made among these three syndromes. Table 1.1 begins our attempt to summarize some of these primary distinctions.

Regarding factors that contribute to TRES, Hensel et al.'s (2015) meta-analysis of 17 risk factors from 38 studies of professionals exposed to employment-related indirect trauma provides important observations. Specifically, results suggested that caseloads, in particular workloads wherein the professional worked more with traumatized than non-traumatized clients, were the strongest risk factor. Personal trauma history, especially when the personal trauma was the same as that of clients, also increased risk. Finally, the presence of work support (i.e., from supervisors and colleagues) and social support (i.e., from family and friends) decreased risk.

Vicarious Trauma McCann and Pearlman (1990), who coined the term "vicarious traumatization," suggest it to be the result of direct and long-term empathetic caregiving for traumatized clients. As a result of this work, the professional's beliefs and thinking change. In the words of Pearlman and Saakvitne (1995, p. 31), VT is defined as "transformation in the inner experience of the therapist that comes about as a result of empathic engagement with client's trauma material." Changes brought about by VT's transformative process result in pervasive long-lasting shifts in

Table 1.1 Distinctions among vicarious trauma, secondary traumatic stress, and compassion fatigue

Employment stress type	Consequence of empathetic engagement	Features
VT	Cognitive alterations in world view	Reduced sense of safety, trust, esteem, intimacy, control
STS	Traumatic stress	Stress reactions similar to PTSD
CF	Loss of the ability to empathize	Behavioral and emotional reactions affect empathetic engagement

cognition that alter how the professional views the world and five fundamental issues: (a) safety, (b) trust, (c) esteem, (d) intimacy, and (e) control (Cieslak et al., 2014; Newell & MacNeil, 2010; Pearlman and Saakvitne (1995); Rauvola et al., 2019). To illustrate the cognitive changes brought about by VT, the following example is offered:

> Shawna, a woman in her early 30s and a mother of two, has been working for six years as a school psychologist in a special school for children who have been removed from their homes due to child abuse. Her evaluations require that she collect detailed information about the nature of a child's traumatic experiences. As a consequence of this vicarious exposure to child abuse, she has become overly protective of her children (not allowing them to leave the home without a parent) and has begun sleeping with a gun on her nightstand. With stories of child sexual abuse on her mind, she is also finding intimacy with her partner to be negatively affected.

Secondary Traumatic Stress Figley (1995) was perhaps the first to reference STS within this context; STS is typically operationalized very similarly to post-traumatic stress disorder (PTSD). Professional assignments that require empathetic understanding of the intense and often horrific experiences of traumatized clients can lead to behaviors, emotions, and cognitions very similar to PTSD (Branson, 2019; Cieslak et al., 2014; National Child Traumatic Stress Network, 2011; Sprang et al., 2019; van der Merwe & Hunt, 2019); the symptoms of which are presented in Table 1.2. In fact, the *Diagnostic and Statistical Manual of Mental Disorders* criteria for PTSD indicate that the trauma exposure (required for PTSD diagnosis) can include "Experiencing repeated or extreme exposure to aversive details of the traumatic event(s) (e.g., first responders collecting human remains; police officers repeatedly exposed to details of child abuse)" (APA, 2013; p. 271). Differentiating it from PTSD, it would appear that STS does not require the trauma exposure to be

Table 1.2 Symptoms of PTSD

Intrusion	Cognition and mood
Intrusive memories	Inability to remember
Nightmares	Negative beliefs/expectations
Flashbacks	Distorted thoughts about the event
Reminders = psychological distress	Negative emotions
Reminders = physiological reactions	Inability to experience positive emotion
	Diminished interest in activities
	Detachment/estrangement
Avoidance	Arousal and reactivity
Avoiding memories, thoughts, feelings	Irritable/angry
Avoiding physical reminders	Reckless/self-destructive
	Hypervigilant
	Easily startled
	Poor concentration
	Sleep difficulties

Note. Adapted from APA (2013)

either "repeated" or "extreme." Thus, a professional may experience STS and not have PTSD (Sprang et al., 2019).

When compared with VT, it would appear that STS places more of an emphasis on the behavioral manifestation of symptoms (with VT focusing less on symptoms of traumatic stress and more on a change in cognitions following cumulative exposure). While VT is more of a process or gradual shift in thinking, STS can occur after a single exposure to traumatic material (NCTSN, 2011). However, as is the case with PTSD, risk of STS increases with chronic exposure to client's trauma narratives. VT and STS may occur together or independently (NCTSN, 2011; Newell & MacNeil, 2010). To illustrate the emotional, behavioral, and cognitive changes brought about by STS, the following example is offered:

> John has been working as a therapist in a veteran's hospital for the past seven years. His focus has been on helping to treat persons suffering from PTSD. His use of trauma-focused cognitive behavioral therapy requires him to help clients develop detailed trauma narratives and facilitate their processing of horrific and incredibly violent traumatic experiences. Over time, John has begun to notice that he has begun to have many of the same symptoms as his clients. For example, he can't stop thinking about their narratives, which have found their way into his dreams. He is feeling detached and estranged from significant others in his life, and has difficulty experiencing positive emotions; he is irritable and often has angry outbursts outside of work and has problems concentrating.

Compassion Fatigue Originally coined by Joinson (1992) and further developed by Figley (1995), CF can be conceptualized as "a function of bearing witness to the suffering of others" (p. 1435), which results in the loss of a caregiver's ability to empathize with clients and others for whom they care (Adams et al., 2006). It has been conceptualized as a unique form of burnout for the caregiving professional (Cieslak et al., 2014). As was illustrated in Fig. 1.1, we conceptualize CF as having substantial overlap with professional burnout, a type of burnout that is influenced by and associated with STS and VT (Adams et al., 2006; Day & Anderson, 2011). Like burnout, the development of CF is a more gradual cumulative process (Rauvola et al., 2019), wherein professional requirements to repeatedly engage with a client's trauma narratives results in increasing levels of STS. From these increasing levels of traumatic stress and resulting CF, the professional enters a "state of tension and preoccupation with the traumatized patients" (Figley, 2002, p. 1435). To illustrate CF, the following example is offered:

> Efren was a close friend and classmate of both Shawna and John. All three were undergraduate psychology majors who specialized in different fields of mental health in graduate school. At a recent college reunion, Efren shared that he has become increasingly "burned-out" by his work at a homeless shelter, and after sharing his experiences, he learned that he was experiencing many of the same reactions as Shawna and John. Efren has an increasing sense that he is not helping his clients and is feeling increasingly hopeless, exhausted, and irritable. From these reactions, he finds it increasingly difficult to focus on client needs and understand their challenges. In fact, he has come to realize that he is finding it difficult to empathize with client challenges (in particular, their traumatic stressors).

Prevalence

Specific prevalence rates associated with various helping professions for burnout and TRES vary (Greinacher et al., 2019; McKinley et al., 2017; van Mol et al., 2015), due in large part to the substantial variability in how these constructs are defined and measured. For example, from a systematic literature review of 182 studies, Rotenstein et al. (2018) reported physician burnout rates varied from 0 to just over 80%. Similarly, van Mol et al. (2015) suggested that among professionals working in intensive care units, STS and CF range from 0% to 38.5% and 7.3% to 40%, respectively. To get a sense of this variability in prevalence estimates for burnout, a PsycINFO database search was conducted using the terms "burnout" and "prevalence." The resulting 1,032 documents were then sorted according to search term relevance. From this relevance listing, in Table 1.3, we selected 28 studies that

Table 1.3 Prevalence (percentage) of burnout within various disciplines

Discipline	Source	Prevalence
Medical students	Mazurkiewicz et al., 2012	71.0
Veterinary technicians	Kogan et al., 2020	58.3
Rescue workers	Chatzea et al., 2018	57.0
Physicians[a]	Kansoun et al., 2019	54.0
Dentists	Aguilera & de Alba Garcia, 2013	52.2
Internal medicine physicians	Doolittle, 2020	52.0
Nurses[a]	Zhang et al., 2018	52.0
Stroke neurologists	Zétola et al., 2019	44.6
Oncology medical residents	Joaquim et al., 2018	42.2
Mental health professionals[a]	O'Conner et al., 2018	40.0
Junior doctors	Toral-Villanueva et al., 2009	40.0
Hospice and palliative care clinicians	Kamal et al., 2020	38.7
Intensive care burn physicians	Haik et al., 2017	38.2
Primary care physicians	Spinelli et al., 2016	37.5
Medical residents	Rodrigues et al., 2018	35.7
Medical residents	Ripp et al., 2010	34.0
NICU nurses, physicians, residents	Tawifk et al. 2017	26.7
First year medical students	Dos Santos Boni et al., 2018	26.4
Emergency nurses[b]	Adriaenssens et al., 2015	26.0
Primary care clinical assistants	Spinelli et al., 2016	24.6
Oncology nurses	Yu et al., 2016	21.14
Military mental health professionals	Kok et al., 2016	20.6
Medical students	Barbosa et al., 2018	12.0
Special education teachers	Gil-Monte et al., 2005	11.7
Nurses[a]	Woo et al., 2020	11.23
Police officers	Quieros et al., 2020	11.0
Teachers	Carlotto & Câmara, 2019	7.5
Pain medicine physicians	Riquelme et al., 2018	7.3

Note. [a]Global estimate from meta-analysis, [b]Global estimate from systematic review

Table 1.4 Prevalence (percentage) of trauma-related stress within various disciplines

Discipline	Stress type	Source	Prevalence
Nurses[a]	CF	Zhang et al., 2018	52.6
Victim advocates	STS	Benuto et al., 2018	50.0
Child protection workers	CF	Conrad & Kellar-Guenther, 2006	49.9
Child protective service workers	STS	Cornille & Meyers, 1999	37.0
Substance abuse therapists	STS	Johansen et al., 2019	22.0
Oncology nurses	CF	Yu et al., 2016	21.4
Alcohol and other drug workers	STS	Ewer et al., 2015	19.9
Mental health providers for military	STS	Cieslak et al., 2013	19.2
Rescue workers	STS	Chatzea et al., 2018	17.1
Social workers	STS	Bride, 2007	15.2
Behavior health providers	CF	Sprang et al., 2007	13.2
Emergency medicine clinicians	STS	Roden-Foreman et al., 2017	12.7
Child abuse investigators	STS	MacEachern et al., 2019	11.0

Note. [a]Global estimate from meta-analysis

provided a single global estimate of burnout generalizable to diverse groups of professional caregivers published in a peer reviewed journal (with special attention given to more recent studies).

Prevalence studies of TRES (i.e., VT, STS, and CF) are much less frequent than studies of burnout (van Mol et al., 2015). Again, to obtain a sense of the variability found in these estimates, separate PsycINFO database searches using the terms "secondary traumatic stress and prevalence," "compassion fatigue and prevalence," and "vicarious trauma and prevalence" were conducted. The result of these three searches was 84, 69, and 32 documents, respectively. Those more recent studies that provided an estimate of employment-related traumatic stress generalizable to a professional caregiving discipline were used to generate the data provided in Table 1.4. Within these studies, it appeared that STS and VT were used interchangeably and there were no studies that provided a prevalence estimate specifically and uniquely connected to VT. Thus, in Table 1.4, we can find a sampling of studies that provided estimates of only CF and STS.

The Consequences of Burnout and Trauma-Related Employment Stress

In the chapters that follow, we will explore how to address the challenges of burnout and TRES. To emphasize the importance of this guidance, in this section, we briefly explore some of the consequences of these work-related challenges. In doing so, we hope to underscore the importance of prevention and early intervention.

Physical

The physical consequences of burnout can be part of a vicious cycle, wherein burn-out's physical consequences (e.g., sleep difficulties) lead to more burnout. Additionally, from their review of the literature, Yang and Hayes (2020) cite studies suggesting that psychotherapist burnout may lead to gastrointestinal symptoms, sleep disturbances, and (especially for professions that involve sitting for extended periods of time) back and neck pain. Similarly, STS is associated with poor physical health including fatigue, gastritis, sleep difficulties, and joint and muscular pain (Colombo et al., 2019; Rizkalla & Segal, 2019).

Psychological

Psychological consequences of burnout include an increased risk for depression, anxiety, and traumatic stress disorders (especially among less experienced workers in their respective fields). Qualitative study has revealed general psychological distress and guilt related to taking time away from work to be associated with burnout. Finally, and not surprisingly, burnout is negatively associated with job satisfaction (Yang & Hayes, 2020). STS is also associated with problems with intimacy, PTSD, anxiety, depression, and somatic complaints (Bober & Regehr, 2006; Colombo et al., 2019; Gärtner et al., 2019; Rizkalla & Segal, 2019).

Organizational

Given the physical and psychological consequences mentioned above, it is not surprising that Yang and Hayes (2020) reported that burnout contributed to job turnover. In addition, it is suggested that burnout among therapists contributes to poor client engagement (clients discontinuing treatment) and to be a predictor of client outcomes.

Purpose and Format of This Book

With this understanding of burnout and TRES in mind, the remainder of this book focuses on prevention and intervention for the impact that empathetic caregiving can have on those in helping roles. As illustrated by Fig. 1.2, the capacity to provide empathetic caregiving, especially to traumatized individuals, is limited and can be conceptualized as water within a glass (with the amount of water symbolizing the capacity to empathize). As caregiving is offered, the water is drained from the glass

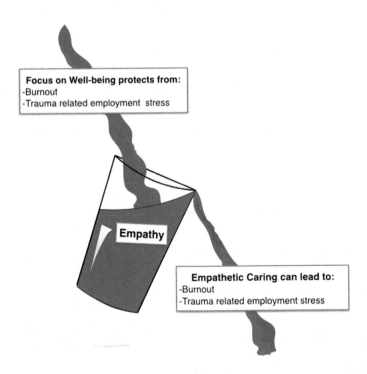

Fig. 1.2 The capacity to provide empathetic caregiving to traumatized clients is finite

and when emptied the capacity to empathize is reduced and burnout and TRES can result. However, to the extent that one is able to access both the internal and external supports needed for this very difficult work, the odds of being able to retain the capacity to offer empathetic caregiving are increased (the glass does not empty).

This book is focused on the technique of acceptance and commitment therapy (ACT) as an intervention to "maintain water in the glass" and both prevent and intervene in burnout and TRES symptoms. The goal of ACT is not to eliminate certain parts of one's experience of life, but rather to learn how to experience life more fully, without as much struggle and with vitality and commitment. Further, goals of ACT include a reduction of suffering, an increase of psychological flexibility, and an increase in one's opportunity to change their behavior and engage in committed action toward their valued goals and outcomes.

This book is geared toward a fairly wide audience, including but not limited to, health providers including physicians, nurses, and veterinarians; mental health providers, such as school psychologists, counselors, clinical psychologists, psychiatrists, and social workers; first responders, such as police officers, firefighters, and emergency medical technicians; military personnel; educators, such as teachers and administrators; and family caregivers, such as parents and others who provide caregiving support to a family member who needs extra support. Table 1.5 summarizes the content of this book.

Table 1.5 Content overview

Chapter 2: Introduction to Acceptance and Commitment Practices
A critical review of literature addressing the use of ACTs in the prevention and intervention of burnout and TRES
Introduction to acceptance and commitment practices, including the primary components of ACT (mindfulness, acceptance, defusion, values, and goal setting).
Overview of acceptance and commitment research as it relates to mental health, burnout, and TRES.
Chapter 3: Mindfulness and Acceptance Practices
Examines mindfulness and acceptance practices as they relate to burnout and TRES.
Specific mindfulness techniques, including practical tools and case examples.
Acceptance practices, including practical tools and case examples.
Easy to use handouts.
Chapter 4: Defusion and Cognitive Techniques
Highlights cognitive techniques, including defusion practices, as they relate to burnout and TRES.
The role of thoughts in stress, trauma, and burnout.
The use of cognitive approaches, including defusion techniques.
Practical tools and case examples.
Easy to use handouts.
Chapter 5: Commitment: Values and Professional Goal Setting
Examines the use of commitment practices as they related to burnout and TRES.
Review of commitment techniques and their importance in working with stress, fatigue, and burnout.
Identifying personal and professional values.
Identifying personal and professional goals.
Practical tools and case examples.
Easy to use handouts.
Chapter 6: Workplace Environments: Buffering Against Compassion Fatigue and Burnout
Examines strategies used in the workplace to help prevent and intervene in burnout and TRES.
Environment and stress.
Managing caseloads.
Strategies to use at work for buffering against compassion fatigue and burnout.
Practical techniques and tips for supporting employees by the workplace.
Chapter 7: Assessment, Resources, and Conclusion
Provides assessment tools for well-being and current symptoms of burnout and TRES, along with helping resources. A summary of the book is also given.
A review of assessments for well-being, compassion fatigue, burnout, stress, depression, STS and VT, and suicide.
Helping resources.
Summary and concluding comments.

Terminology: Practitioner, Client, TRES, and Non-gendered Language

Throughout this book several key terms and pronouns are utilized. Specifically, the terms "practitioner," "client," and "TRES" are used, along with non-gendered language to refer to individuals or groups. The term "practitioner" is meant to encompass anyone who engages in the practice of mindfulness or acceptance techniques and engages in such techniques to teach or train another individual or group in that practice. The term "client" refers to anyone whom the caregiver serves, whether it be a patient, a student, an animal, the owner of an animal, or their own family member. The term "TRES" is used throughout the book to encompass the areas of VT, STS, and CF. Finally, non-gendered language is used, with the pronouns of they/them/their utilized as opposed to he/him/his or she/her/hers, as is consistent with inclusive language.

References

Adams, R. E., Boscarino, J. A., & Figley, C. R. (2006). Compassion fatigue and psychological distress among social workers: A validation study. *American Journal of Orthopsychiatry, 76*(1), 103–108. https://doi.org/10.1037/0002-9432.76.1.103.

Adriaenssens, J., De Gucht, V., & Maes, S. (2015). Determinants and prevalence of burnout in emergency nurses: A systematic review of 25 years of research. *International Journal of Nursing Studies, 52*(2), 649–661. https://doi.org/10.1016/j.ijnurstu.2014.11.004

American Psychiatric Association. (2013). *Diagnostic and statistical manual of mental disorders* (5th ed.). https://doi.org/10.1176/appi.books.9780890425596.

Barak, M. E. M., Nissly, J. A., & Levin, A. (2001). Antecedents to retention and turnover among child welfare, social work, and other human service employees: What can we learn from past research? A review and metanalysis. *Social Service Review, 75*(4), 625–661. http://www.jstor.com/stable/10.1086/32316.

Barbosa, M. L., Rodrigues Ferreira, B. L., Vargas, T. N., Ney da Silva, G. M., Nardi, A. E., Machado, S., & Caixeta, L. (2018). Burnout prevalence and associated factors among Brazilian medical students. *Clinical Practice and Epidemiology in Mental Health, 14*, 188–195. https://doi.org/10.2174/1745017901814010188

Benuto, L. T., Newlands, R., Ruork, A., Hooft, S., & Ahrendt, A. (2018). Secondary traumatic stress among victim advocates: Prevalence and correlates. *Journal of Evidence-Informed Social Work, 15*(5), 494–509. https://doi.org/10.1080/23761407.2018.1474825

Bober, T., & Regehr, C. (2006). Strategies for reducing secondary or vicarious trauma: Do they work? *Brief Treatment and Crisis Intervention, 6*(1), 1–9. https://doi.org/10.1093/brief-treatment/mhj001.

Branson, D. C. (2019). Vicarious trauma, themes in research, and terminology: A review of literature. *Traumatology, 25*(1), 2–10. https://doi.org/10.1037/trm0000161.

Bride, B. E. (2007). Prevalence of secondary traumatic stress among social workers. *Social Work, 52*(1), 63–70. https://doi.org/10.1093/sw/52.1.63

Carlotto, M. S., & Câmara, S. G. (2019). Prevalence and predictors of burnout syndrome among public elementary school teachers. *Análise Psicológica, 37*(2), 135–146. https://doi.org/10.14417/ap.1471

Chatzea, V. E., Sifaki-Pistolla, D., Vlachaki, S. A., Melidoniotis, E., & Pistolla, G. (2018). PTSD, burnout and well-being among rescue workers: Seeking to understand the impact of the European refugee crisis on rescuers. *Psychiatry Research, 262,* 446–451. https://doi.org/10.1016/j.psychres.2017.09.022

Cieslak, R., Anderson, V., Bock, J., Moore, B. A., Peterson, A. L., & Benight, C. C. (2013). Secondary traumatic stress among mental health providers working with the military: Prevalence and its work- and exposure-related correlates. *Journal of Nervous and Mental Disorders, 201*(11), 917–925. https://doi.org/10.1097/NMD.0000000000000034

Cieslak, R., Shoji, K., Douglas, A., Melville, E., Luszczynska, A., & Benight, C. C. (2014). A meta-analysis of the relationship between job burnout and secondary traumatic stress among workers with indirect exposure to trauma. *Psychological Services, 11*(1), 75–86. https://doi.org/10.1037/a0033798.

Colombo, L., Emanuel, F., & Zito, M. (2019). Secondary traumatic stress: Relationship with symptoms, exhaustion, and emotions among cemetery workers. *Frontiers in Psychology, 10,* 1–11. https://doi.org/10.3389/fpsyg.2019.00633.

Conrad, D., & Kellar-Guenther, Y. (2006). Compassion fatigue, burnout, and compassion satisfaction among Colorado child protection workers. *Child Abuse & Neglect, 30*(10), 1071–1080. https://doi.org/10.1016/j.chiabu.2006.03.009

Cornille, T. A., & Meyers, T. W. (1999). Secondary traumatic stress among child protective service workers: Prevalence, severity and predictive factors. *Traumatology, 5*(1), 15–31. https://doi.org/10.1177/153476569900500105

Day, J. R., & Anderson, R. A. (2011). Compassion fatigue: An application of the concept to informal caregivers of family members with dementia. *Nursing Research and Practice, 2011,* 1–10. https://doi.org/10.1155/2011/408024.

Doolittle, B. R. (2020). Association of burnout with emotional coping strategies, friendship, and institutional support among internal medicine physicians. *Journal of Clinical Psychology in Medical Settings.* https://doi.org/10.1007/s10880-020-09724-6

Dos Santos Boni, R. A., Paiva, C. E., De Oliveira, M. A., Lucchetti, G., Guerreiro Fregnani, J. H. T., & Ribeiro Paiva, B. S. (2018). Burnout among medical students during the first years of undergraduate school: Prevalence and associated factors. *PLoS One, 13*(3). https://doi.org/10.1371/journal.pone.0191746

Ewer, P. L., Teesson, M., Sannibale, C., Roche, A., & Mills, K. L. (2015). The prevalence and correlates of secondary traumatic stress among alcohol and other drug workers in Australia. *Drug and Alcohol Review, 34*(3), 252–258. https://doi.org/10.1111/dar.12204

Figley, C. (1995). Compassion fatigue as secondary traumatic stress disorder: An overview. In C. Figley (Ed.), *Compassion fatigue: Coping with secondary traumatic stress disorder in those who treat the traumatized* (pp. 1–20). Brunner/Mazel.

Figley, C. (2002). Compassion fatigue: Psychotherapists' chronic lack of self care. *Psychotherapy in Practice, 58*(11), 1433–1441. https://doi.org/10.1002/jclp.10090.

Gärtner, A., Behnke, A., Conrad, D., Kolassa, I.-T., & Rojas, R. (2019). Emotion regulation in rescue workers: Differential relationship with perceived work-related stress and stress-related symptoms. *Frontiers in Psychology, 9,* 1–12. https://doi.org/10.3389/fpsyg.2018.02744.

Gil-Monte, P. R., Carretero, N., Roldán, M. D., & Núñez-Román, E. M. (2005). Prevalencia del síndrome de quemarse por el trabajo en monitores de taller para personas con discapacidad [Burnout prevalence amongst instructors of disabled people]. *Revista de Psicología Del Trabajo y de Las Organizaciones, 21*(1–2), 107–123. https://www.redalyc.org/articulo.oa?id=231317039007

Greinacher, A., Derezza-Greeven, C., Herzog, W., & Nikendei, C. (2019). Secondary traumatization in first responders: A systematic review. *European Journal of Psychotraumatology, 10*(1), 2–21. https://doi.org/10.1080/20008198.2018.1562840.

Haik, J., Brown, S., Liran, A., Visentin, D., Sokolov, A., Zilinsky, I., & Kornhaber, R. (2017). Burnout and compassion fatigue: Prevalence and associations among Israeli burn clinicians. *Neuropsychiatric Disease and Treatment, 13*, 1533–1530. https://doi.org/10.2147/NDT.S133181

Hensel, J. M., Ruiz, C., Finney, C., & Dewa, C. S. (2015). Meta-analysis of risk factors for secondary traumatic stress in therapeutic work with trauma victims. *Journal of Traumatic Stress, 28*(2), 83–91. https://doi.org/10.1002/jts.21998.

Joaquim, A., Custódio, S., Savva-Bordalo, J., Chacim, S., Carvalhais, I., Lombo, L., Lopes, H., Araújo, A., & Gomes, R. (2018). Burnout and occupational stress in the medical residents of oncology, haematology and radiotherapy: A prevalence and predictors study in Portugal. *Psychology, Health & Medicine, 23*(3), 317–324. https://doi.org/10.1080/1354850 6.2017.1344256

Johansen, A. B., Kristiansen, E., Bjelland, I., & Tavakoli, S. (2019). Secondary traumatic stress in Norwegian SUD- therapists: Symptoms and related factors. *NAT Nordisk Alkohol & Narkotikatidskrift, 36*(6), 522–531. https://doi.org/10.1177/1455072519847014

Joinson, C. (1992). Coping with compassion fatigue. *Nursing, 22*(4), 116–121. https://doi.org/10.1097/00152193-199204000-00035.

Kamal, A. H., Bull, J. H., Wolf, S. P., Swetz, K. M., Shanafelt, T. D., Ast, K., Kavalieratos, D., & Sinclair, C. T. (2020). Prevalence and predictors of burnout among hospice and palliative care clinicians in the US. *Journal of Pain and Symptom Management, 59*(5), e6–e13. https://doi.org/10.1016/j.jpainsymman.2019.11.017

Kansoun, Z., Boyer, L., Hodgkinson, M., Villes, V., Lançon, C., & Fond, G. (2019). Burnout in French physicians: A systematic review and meta-analysis. *Journal of Affective Disorders, 246*, 132–147. https://doi.org/10.1016/j.jad.2018.12.056

Kirsch, D. L. (2019, May 28). *"Burnout syndrome" has been recognized for the first time as an official medical diagnosis*. The American Institute of Stress. https://www.stress.org/burnout-is-now-an-official-medical-condition

Kogan, L. R., Wallace, J. E., Schoenfeld-Tacher, R., Hellyer, P. W., & Richards, M. (2020). Veterinary technicians and occupational burnout. *Frontiers in Veterinary Science, 7*, 1–9. https://doi.org/10.3389/fvets.2020.00328

Kok, B. C., Herrell, R. K., Grossman, S. H., West, J. C., & Wilk, J. E. (2016). Prevalence of professional burnout among military mental health service providers. *Psychiatric Services, 67*(1), 137–140. https://doi.org/10.1176/appi.ps.201400430

Lerias, D., & Byrne, M. K. (2003). Vicarious traumatization: Symptoms and predictors. *Stress and Health: Journal of the International Society for the Investigation of Stress, 19*(3), 129–138. https://doi.org/10.1002/smi.969.

Lloyd, C., King, R., & Chenoweth, L. (2002). Social work, stress and burnout: A review. *Journal of Mental Health, 11*(3), 255–266. https://doi.org/10.1080/09638230020023642.

MacEachern, A. D., Dennis, A. A., Jackson, S., & Jindal-Snape, D. (2019). Secondary traumatic stress: Prevalence and symptomology amongst detective officers investigating child protection cases. *Journal of Police and Criminal Psychology, 34*, 165–174. https://doi.org/10.1007/s11896-018-9277-x

Maslach, C., & Leiter, M. P. (2016). Understanding the burnout experience: Recent research and its implications for psychiatry. *World Psychiatry, 15*(2), 103–111. https://doi.org/10.1002/wps.20311.

Mazurkiewicz, R., Korenstein, D., Fallar, R., & Ripp, J. (2012). The prevalence and correlations of medical student burnout in the pre-clinical years: A cross-sectional study. *Psychology, Health & Medicine, 17*(2), 188–195. https://doi.org/10.1080/13548506.2011.597770

McCann, I. L., & Pearlman, L. A. (1990). Vicarious traumatization: A framework for understanding the psychological effects of working with victims. *Journal of Traumatic Stress, 3*(1), 131–149. https://doi.org/10.1007/BF00975140.

McKinley, T. F., Boland, K. A., & Mahan, J. D. (2017). Burnout and interventions in pediatric residency: A literature review. *Burnout Research, 6*(2017), 9–17. https://doi.org/10.1016/j.burn.2017.02.003.

Montero-Marín, J., Skapinakis, P., Araya, R., Gili, M., & García-Campayo, J. (2011). Towards a brief definition of burnout syndrome by subtypes: Development of the "Burnout Clinical Subtypes Questionnaire" (BCSQ-12). *Health and Quality of Life Outcomes, 9*(74), 1–12. https://doi.org/10.1186/1477-7525-9-74.

Montero-Marín, J., Zubiaga, F., Cereceda, M., Demarzo, M. M. P., Trenc, P., & Garcia-Campayo, J. (2016). Burnout subtypes and absence of self-compassion in primary healthcare professionals: A cross-sectional study. *PLoS One, 11*(6), 1–17. https://doi.org/10.1371/journal.pone.0157499.

National Child Traumatic Stress Network. (2011). *Secondary traumatic stress: A fact sheet for child-serving professionals.* https://www.nctsn.org/resources/secondary-traumatic-stress-fact-sheet-child-serving-professionals

Newell, J. M., & MacNeil, G. A. (2010). Professional burnout, vicarious trauma, secondary traumatic stress, and compassion fatigue: A review of theoretical terms, risk factors, and preventive methods for clinicians and researchers. *Best Practices in Mental Health: An International Journal, 6*(2), 57–68. https://thedavidfollmergroup.com/best-practices-in-mental-health/.

Nimmo, A., & Huggard, P. (2013). A systematic review of the measurement of compassion fatigue, vicarious trauma, and secondary traumatic stress in physicians. *Australasian Journal of Disaster and Trauma Studies, 2013*(1), 37–44. http://trauma.massey.ac.nz/issues/2013-1/AJDTS_2013-1_Nimmo.pdf.

O'Connor, K., Neff, D. M., & Pitman, S. (2018). Burnout in mental health professionals: A systematic review and meta-analysis of prevalence and determinants. *European Psychiatry, 53*, 74–99. https://doi.org/10.1016/j.eurpsy.2018.06.003

Perlman, B., & Hartman, E. A. (1982). Burnout: Summary and future research. *Human Relations, 35*(4), 283–305. https://doi.org/10.1177/001872678203500402

Pearlman, L. A., & Saakvitne, K. (1995). *Trauma and the therapist: Countertransference and vicarious traumatization in psychotherapy with incest survivors.* W.W. Norton.

Queirós, C., Passos, F., Bártolo, A., Marques, A. J., da Silva, C. F., & Pereira, A. (2020). Burnout and stress measurement in police officers: Literature review and a study with the operational police stress questionnaire. *Frontiers in Psychology, 11*, 1–23. https://doi.org/10.3389/fpsyg.2020.00587

Rauvola, R. S., Vega, D. M., & Lavigne, K. N. (2019). Compassion fatigue, secondary traumatic stress, and vicarious traumatization: A qualitative review and research agenda. *Occupational Health Science, 3*(3), 297–336. https://doi.org/10.1007/s41542-019-00045-1.

Ripp, J., Fallar, R., Babyatsky, M., David, R., Reich, L., & Korenstein, D. (2010). Prevalence of resident burnout at the start of training. *Teaching and Learning in Medicine, 22*(3), 172–175. https://doi.org/10.1080/10401334.2010.488194

Riquelme, I., Chacón, J. I., Gándara, A. V., Muro, I., Traseira, S., Monsalve, V., & Soriano, J. F. (2018). Prevalence of burnout among pain medicine physicians and its potential effect upon clinical outcomes in patients with oncologic pain or chronic pain of nononcologic origin. *Pain Medicine, 19*(12), 2398–2407. https://doi.org/10.1093/pm/pnx335

Rizkalla, N., & Segal, S. P. (2019). Trauma during humanitarian work: The effects on intimacy, wellbeing and PTSD-symptoms. *European Journal of Psychotraumatology, 10*(1), 1–12. https://doi.org/10.1080/20008198.2019.1679065.

Roden-Foreman, J. W., Bennett, M. M., Rainey, E. E., Garrett, J. S., Powers, M. B., & Warren, A. M. (2017). Secondary traumatic stress in emergency medicine clinicians. *Cognitive Behaviour Therapy, 46*(6), 522–532. https://doi.org/10.1080/16506073.2017.1315612

Rodrigues, H., Cobucci, R., Oliveira, A., Cabral, J. V., Medeiros, L., Gurgel, K., Souza, T., & Gonçalves, A. K. (2018). Burnout syndrome among medical residents: A systematic review and meta-analysis. *PLoS One, 13*(11). https://doi.org/10.1371/journal.pone.0206840

Rotenstein, L. S., Torre, M., Ramos, M. A., Rosales, R. C., Guille, C., Sen, S., & Mata, D. A. (2018). Prevalence of burnout among physicians: A systematic review. *JAMA: Journal of the American Medical Association, 320*(11), 1131–1150. https://doi.org/10.1001/jama.2018.12777.

Rupert, P. A., Miller, A. O., & Dorociak, K. E. (2015). Preventing burnout: What does the research tell us? *Professional Psychology: Research and Practice, 46*(3), 168–174. https://doi. org/10.1037/a0039297.

Spinelli, W. M., Fernstrom, K. M., Galos, D. L., & Britt, H. R. (2016). Extending our understanding of burnout and its associated factors: Providers and staff in primary care clinics. *Evaluation & the Health Professions, 39*(3), 282–298. https://doi.org/10.1177/0163278716637900

Sprang, G., Clark, J., & Whitt-Woosley, A. (2007). Compassion fatigue, compassion satisfaction, and burnout: Factors impacting a professional's quality of life. *Journal of Loss & Trauma, 12*(3), 259–280. https://doi.org/10.1080/15325020701238093

Sprang, G., Ford, J., Kerig, P., & Bride, B. (2019). Defining secondary traumatic stress and developing targeted assessments and interventions: Lessons learned from research and leading experts. *Traumatology, 25*(2), 72–81. https://doi.org/10.1037/trm0000180.

Tawfk, D. S., Phibbs, C. S., Sexton, J. B., Kan, P., Sharek, P. J., Nisbet, C. C., Rigdon, J., Trockel, M., & Proft, J. (2017). Factors associated with provider burnout in the NICU. *Pediatrics, 139*(5), 1–9. https://doi.org/10.1542/peds.2016-4134

Toral-Villanueva, R., Aguilar-Madrid, G., & Juárez-Pérez, C. A. (2009). Burnout and patient care in junior doctors in Mexico City. *Occupational Medicine, 59*(1), 8–13. https://doi.org/10.1093/occmed/kqn122

van der Merwe, A., & Hunt, X. (2019). Secondary trauma among trauma researchers: Lessons from the field. *Psychological Trauma: Theory, Research, Practice, and Policy, 11*(1), 10–18. https://doi.org/10.1037/tra0000414.

van Mol, M. M. C., Kompanje, E. J. O., Benoit, D. D., Bakker, J., & Nijkamp, M. D. (2015). The prevalence of compassion fatigue and burnout among healthcare professionals in intensive care units: A systematic review. *PLoS One, 10*(8). https://doi.org/10.1371/journal.pone.0136955.

Vlăduţ, C. I., & Kállay, É. (2010). Work stress, personal life, and burnout: Causes, consequences, possible remedies—A theoretical review. *Cognition, Brain, Behavior: An Interdisciplinary Journal, 14*(3), 261–280. https://www.scimagojr.com/journalsearch.php?q=21100860060&tip=sid&clean=0.

Woo, T., Ho, R., Tang, A., & Tam, W. (2020). Global prevalence of burnout symptoms among nurses: A systematic review and meta-analysis. *Journal of Psychiatric Research, 123*, 9–20. https://doi.org/10.1016/j.jpsychires.2019.12.015

World Health Organization. (2019). QD85 Burn-out. *ICD-11 for Mortality and morbidity statistics.* https://icd.who.int/browse11/l-m/en#/http://id.who.int/icd/entity/129180281

Yang, Y., & Hayes, J. A. (2020). Causes and consequences of burnout among mental health professionals: A practice-oriented review of recent empirical literature. *Psychotherapy, 57*(3), 426–436. https://doi.org/10.1037/pst0000317.

Yu, H., Jiang, A., & Shen, J. (2016). Prevalence and predictors of compassion fatigue, burnout and compassion satisfaction among oncology nurses: A cross-sectional survey. *International Journal of Nursing Studies, 57*, 28–38. https://doi.org/10.1016/j.ijnurstu.2016.01.012

Zétola, V. F., Pavanelli, G. M., Pereira, G. U., Germiniani, F. M. B., & Lange, M. C. (2019). Burnout syndrome: Are stroke neurologists at a higher risk? *Arquivos de Neuro-Psiquiatria, 77*(2), 84–90. https://doi.org/10.1590/0004-282x20190002

Zhang, Y. Y., Han, W. L., Qin, W., Yin, H. X., Zhang, C. F., Kong, C., & Wang, Y. L. (2018). Extent of compassion satisfaction, compassion fatigue and burnout in nursing: A meta-analysis. *Journal of Nursing Management, 26*(7), 810–819. https://doi.org/10.1111/jonm.12589

Chapter 2
Introduction to Acceptance and Commitment Practices

Over the last three decades, a number of multifaceted therapies, categorized as "third-wave behavior therapies" (O'Brien et al., 2008. p. 15), have been developed for use with a variety of presenting concerns. These therapies have integrated behavioral, cognitive, and mindfulness techniques to work together under a single model. One such third-wave therapy is called Acceptance and Commitment Therapy (ACT). ACT is an approach based on cognitive-behavioral therapy that incorporates mindfulness and acceptance practices designed to help participants move toward values-oriented goals. Whereas more traditional cognitive-behavioral modalities suggest that change occurs through cognitively reinterpreting the meaning of the stimulus, ACT employs an acceptance approach combined with mindful awareness that helps to increase psychological flexibility (Hayes et al., 2012). Psychological flexibility is achieved by having contact with the present moment and changing or persisting in behaviors when doing so serves to achieve goals that are valued by the individual (Hayes et al., 2006). As is introduced later in this chapter, ACT is an effective intervention for a variety of presenting concerns, including burnout and trauma-related employment stress (TRES).

Components of Acceptance and Commitment Therapy

There are six overlapping and synergistic processes in ACT referred to as the "hexaflex" (Hayes et al., 2012). These core processes are: (a) attention to the present moment, (b) cognitive defusion, (c) acceptance, (d) self-as-context, (e) values, and (f) committed action. Together, these processes aid in increasing our psychological flexibility or the ability to be in the present moment, with full awareness and openness to the experience and with our goals and actions guided by our values (Harris, 2009). By being aware and accepting of our experiences and by acting according to our values, we can experience a greater sense of meaning and quality of life. The six areas of ACT are briefly defined below in Table 2.1 and the following paragraphs.

M. L. Holland et al., *Burnout and Trauma Related Employment Stress*,
https://doi.org/10.1007/978-3-030-83492-0_2

Table 2.1 The six components of ACT

Component	Definition
Attention to the present moment	Mindfully and flexibly living in the here and now
Cognitive defusion	The ability to separate or create distance from our thoughts
Acceptance	The voluntary adoption of taking an intentionally open, flexible, receptive, and nonjudgmental posture toward the present-moment experience
Self-as-context	Having awareness of our own awareness or the observing mind or self that is aware that it is having thoughts
Values	Chosen life directions
Committed action	Turning values into committed patterns of action, namely, short-term to long-term goals

In the ACT model, *attention to the present moment* is an awareness process, rather than a thinking process and involves being open to the present moment, even if the present moment involves discomfort and suffering. Practitioners assume that the past and future are stories we create in our minds. In reality, the past is gone forever, and the future is yet to come. Nevertheless, these stories can be so distracting that we miss what is actually going on in the present moment. Time, in the ACT models, is only a measure of change, and there is only the now from which to work to create that change (Hayes et al., 2012).

The idea of *cognitive defusion* in the ACT model is to counter the process wherein our thoughts dominate our behaviors and experiences (Harris, 2009). We have an automatic ability to translate experiences, such as events, feelings, and ideas, into words; a process Hayes (2005) coins "the word machine." Our minds are constantly comparing, evaluating, planning, and predicting. This use of language most likely initially evolved as a form of social control and cooperation between humans as a danger signaling tool to keep us safe and alive, until it gradually expanded into a more general and diffuse process (Hayes et al., 2012). This process eventually facilitated negative thinking patterns, causing us to label others, the world, and ourselves in unhealthy or destructive ways. It is the process wherein our thoughts dominate our behaviors and our experiences. Often we get stuck in rule-bound living, fixating on the belief that there is only one right and true answer to any given question. This can, obviously, become problematic to our mental health and flexibility in living. When we create distance in our awareness from our thoughts, we can begin to recognize them for what they are – just thoughts. With this recognition, we can access more choices for how we respond and behave (Harris, 2009).

In the ACT model, *acceptance* is an alternative to avoiding or trying to block thoughts and feelings, which can actually maintain and escalate the distress, also known as experiential avoidance (Hayes et al., 2012). It is important to note that acceptance is a process by which we become willing to turn toward things as they really are, not a giving-up or giving-in experience (Hayes, 2005). This can, in turn, allow for informed choice in decisions, as opposed to feeling stuck or avoidant in the resistance of reality.

The "observing self" or the "I" in our awareness is considered *self-as-context*. It is our self-description, including our thoughts, feelings, memories, judgments, and ideas about our identities (Hayes et al., 2012). Whereas self-as-awareness is the process of noticing and being in the present moment, self-as-context is the part of the self that is *doing the noticing*. In ACT, self-as-context can facilitate cognitive defusion and acceptance as, once we have understood the concept of the observing self, we can better understand how to simply observe and accept our feelings and thoughts (Harris, 2009; Hayes et al., 2012).

Guiding principles, or *values,* provide us direction in our actions and behaviors. They are distinct and separate from wants, needs, morals, virtues, ethics, and goals. Harris (2009) defines five key points about values in the ACT model: (a) values are in the here and now, (b) they never need to be justified, (c) they often need to be prioritized, (d) they are best held lightly, and (e) they are freely chosen. The first point is that we live according to our values in the present moment and that it is never too late to begin living in a way that is consistent with our values. Secondly, values are unique and individual to each person and reflect what is meaningful to that person. Because of this, we do not need to justify our values. The third point indicates that certain values may take priority over others, depending on the situation or phase of life we are in. Values are best held lightly; when fusion occurs with values, they may begin to feel restrictive and oppressive, like commandments or rules that must be obeyed. Finally, we choose to act according to our values because they matter to us, thereby making our values freely chosen.

Commitment to action is the component of ACT that builds a road map toward our goals, or certain things we want to have or achieve. Specific action steps are identified toward creating a vital and values-based life (Hayes, 2005). An important element of *committed action* is the ability to identify barriers that may arise and how to use cognitive defusion, acceptance, and mindfulness to overcome those barriers (Harris, 2009).

Taken together, the six components of ACT can assist the individual in addressing the challenges of burnout and TRES. A common thread throughout burnout, compassion fatigue, vicarious trauma, and secondary traumatic stress is that the individual seeks relief from their symptoms by turning away from or avoiding what is causing the pain. For example, skipping work, socially isolating, and using unhealthy coping strategies, such as drinking alcohol excessively, are all avoidance tactics. However, this turning away from the pain often also includes the individual turning away from the areas of life that they value and, subsequently, their goals. In ACT, the provider helps the individual to reaffirm their values and goals in a mindful, observing, present-moment way, allowing the individual to expose themselves to the painful situation so that they no longer avoid the issue. Through metaphors and therapeutic exercises, the individual learns to see the content of the pain and the thoughts driving the discomfort in a less fused, more flexible way. This allows the individual to respond differently to their thoughts, thereby increasing acceptance and decreasing avoidance and/or feelings of being overwhelmed by the pain. This is

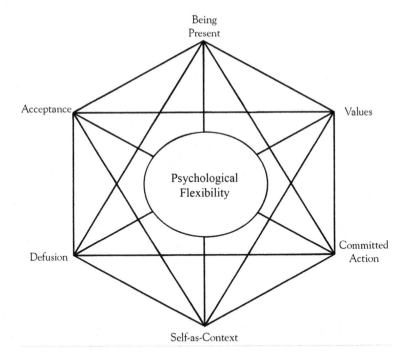

Fig. 2.1 Hexaflex model of ACT. (Copyright Steven C. Hayes. Used by permission)

termed as increasing psychological flexibility in the theory of ACT, a visual representation of such is offered in Fig. 2.1. In the next section, we review ACT's empirical supports, first as it relates to general mental health, then specifically as it addresses the symptoms of burnout and trauma related employment stress.

Research Support for Acceptance and Commitment Therapy (ACT)

The use of ACT has been well documented over the last several decades for its use with youth and adult populations. This section reviews research supporting the use of ACT in addressing anxiety, depression, and health problems/pain, in addition to promoting general well-being.

Anxiety

ACT has been used as a therapeutic intervention for anxiety in both youth and adults (Bluett et al., 2014; Greco et al., 2005; Hancock et al., 2016). From their meta-analysis, Bluett et al. (2014) suggest that ACT is equally effective as manualized treatments, such as CBT, when treating anxiety. In a study of 128 individuals with diagnoses of one or more anxiety disorders, those that participated in either the CBT or ACT intervention groups improved similarly across all outcomes from pre- to post-treatment. A follow-up assessment of subjects who participated in ACT showed more significant improvements in their anxiety than those in the CBT group ($p < 0.05$, $d = 1.26$; Arch et al., 2012). Additionally, patients who were referred to treatment for severe health anxiety significantly improved after participating in group therapy using ACT as the orientation (Eilenberg et al., 2016).

Depression

Twohig and Levin (2017), in summarizing 36 randomized control trial studies, found that ACT is more efficacious than wait-list control conditions and other forms of treatment, with relatively equivalent effects to CBT for depression. Through their analysis, treatment outcomes appeared to be primarily mediated through increases in psychological flexibility. In a study by Forman et al. (2007), over 100 outpatient participants reporting moderate to severe levels of depression or anxiety were randomly assigned to either a traditional cognitive therapy or to an ACT treatment. Both groups, after treatment, evidenced large, equivalent improvements in depression and anxiety, among other variables (e.g., self-reported quality of life indicators). However, the mechanisms of action appeared to differ. In the cognitive group, changes in "observing" and "describing" one's experiences appeared to mediate outcomes, whereas in the ACT group "acting with awareness," "experiential avoidance," and "acceptance" mediated treatment outcomes. Najvani et al. (2015) found in their study of depression in women diagnosed with breast cancer that, after an eight session ACT group, significant improvements in depression (as measured by the *Beck Depression Inven*tory) and psychological flexibility (as measured by the *Acceptance and Action Questionnaire-II*; AAQ-II) were found as compared with the control group. The researchers contended that increasing acceptance and mindfulness processes, along with behavioral change, increased the participant's psychological flexibility, which in turn improved their mood. Feros et al. (2011) concurs; ACT intervention evidencing changes in psychological flexibility predicts improvement in mood and distress.

Chronic Pain

Individuals with chronic pain also respond positively to ACT, with the mediating processes found to be similar to those documented in studies with depression and anxiety. For example, among youth suffering from debilitating chronic pain, variables consistent with psychological flexibility mediated the effects of ACT-based interventions to reduce pain intensity (Wicksell et al., 2007; Wicksell et al., 2011). Psychological flexibility in the context of chronic pain means that attention is focused on the opportunities of the current situation rather than on ruminating about the past or worrying about the future; sensations, thoughts, and feelings are accepted, and behavior is focused on realizing valued goals instead of focusing on pain control (McCracken & Vowles, 2014). These improvements occur through changes in both pain impairment beliefs and resulting reductions in pain reactivity, predominantly through acceptance and psychological flexibility, rather than through changes in self-efficacy, cognitive catastrophizing, or actual pain relief (Wicksell et al., 2011). Similarly, in what might be considered a more comprehensive study, Scott et al. (2016) examined changes in processes of psychological flexibility following an ACT-based treatment for chronic pain in adults. Significant improvements were observed from pre-, post-, and follow-up assessment on measures of functioning, including depression, pain acceptance and intensity, cognitive fusion, and committed action. Regression analyses indicated that the change in participant's psychological flexibility processes cumulatively explained 6%–27% of the variance in changes in depression and overall functioning over both post- and follow-up assessment periods.

In 2016, Veehof et al. conducted a meta-analysis of 28 studies to assess the effectiveness of acceptance and mindfulness-based interventions for chronic pain patients across randomized control trials. Of interest is the result that ACT intervention had a statistically significant higher mean effect on depression and anxiety than mindfulness-based intervention, though when compared with traditional CBT, the differences were not statistically significant. ACT also appears to hold promise for those suffering from chronic fatigue syndrome, primarily stemming from increases in patient psychological flexibility (Jonsjö et al., 2019). Overall, these studies and reviews indicate that ACT can effectively lead to improved health outcomes.

Overall Well-Being

It appears that there are several factors associated with ACT most related to increases in well-being, including increasing participants' psychological flexibility and the use of mindfulness. Increases in psychological flexibility are key in increasing mood and overall well-being (Twohig & Levin, 2017), with psychological flexibility being defined as increasing acceptance and decreasing avoidance and/or feelings of being overwhelmed by life circumstances. Mindfulness can play a critical role in moving toward this flexibility, in addition to fostering overall psychological health. In a systematic review of the literature by Emerson et al. (2017), 12 studies of mindfulness intervention lent support for overall participant gains in emotional regulation and self-compassion and reduced self-reported stress. In a study of mindfulness with pre-service teachers, Kerr et al. (2017) found post-intervention mindfulness participants reported greater emotional clarity and improved regulation of negative emotions as compared with the control group. In addition, within-group differences suggested that mindfulness training helped participants respond more flexibly to stressful emotions. In another study, participants in a mindfulness group reported significant gains in self-regulation, self-compassion, and mindfulness-related skills (observation, nonjudgmental, and nonreacting). Significant improvements in multiple dimensions of sleep quality were found as well (Frank et al., 2015). These findings provide promising evidence of the effectiveness of ACT, particularly the components of psychological flexibility and mindfulness, as a strategy to promote general well-being.

Burnout and ACT

As discussed in Chap. 1, burnout can have considerable individual effects including psychological and physical consequences and negative organizational outcomes such as absenteeism, increased turnover, and decreased job performance of the burned-out employee (Maslach & Leiter, 2016). ACT has been found to be one approach that can help to protect against and intervene in the symptoms of burnout.

In examining careers in the helping professions wherein burnout is prevalent, healthcare providers (e.g., doctors, nurses, veterinarians, and therapists), educators (e.g., principals and teachers), and law enforcement/emergency care officers top the list (American Veterinary Medical Association [AVMA], n.d.; Elwood et al., 2011; Hinds et al., 2015; Lautieri, 2020). ACT has been employed in many of these career sectors and found to be efficacious in ameliorating burnout symptoms. For example, in a study by Donaldson and Bond (2004), participants were studied to determine the effect of acceptance on job satisfaction and well-being. Results found that acceptance of one's thoughts and feelings had greater benefits for mental well-being than attempting to consciously regulate them. In a review of the literature, ACT was found to increase teachers' psychological flexibility, which can aid in decreased experiential avoidance and higher levels of acceptance of circumstances and a feeling of effectiveness (all highly related to areas of burnout; Biglan et al., 2013). Jeffcoat and Hayes (2012) examined the use of ACT bibliotherapy with K-12 school personnel and found that participants who read an ACT book for 2 months showed significant improvement in psychological health, including reduced stress, anxiety, and depressive symptoms, as compared with the wait-list control group. Reducing teacher stress and improving well-being are key components to prevention and early intervention in burnout. Other studies concur that ACT is an effective tool in increasing psychological flexibility and decreasing experiential avoidance, stress, and burnout in teachers (Hinds et al., 2015; Lloyd et al., 2013). For nurses, similar findings have been noted. Specifically, nurses who are more prone to burnout due to care-providing tend to have more psychological inflexibility. Increasing psychological flexibility in nurses can aid in buffering against burnout symptoms (Duarte & Pinto-Gouveia, 2017). When used with social workers, ACT techniques were also found to significantly decrease levels of stress and burnout, along with increasing general mental health, compared with a wait-list control group (Brinkborg et al., 2011). Additionally, a one-day ACT workshop provided to substance abuse counselors evidenced greater decreases in therapist burnout relative to a control group at follow-up (Hayes, 2004). An ACT-based program called Mindfulness for Pain and Performance Enhancement (MPPE) was designed to help Navy recruits effectively manage pain and support their physical recovery, completion of boot camp, and entrance into the Navy. Results indicated the two-week program assisted injury recovery and passing training requirements for graduation. Specifically, results showed a mild reduction in anxiety and experiential avoidance; moderate improvements in pain acceptance, cognitive flexibility, mindfulness, and depression; and large improvements in pain reduction (Udell et al., 2018).

In addition to psychological flexibility, mindfulness has also been found to be a key component of ACT that can be used as an intervention for burnout. In a study by Roeser et al. (2013), results revealed that participants who had engaged in an eight-week, 11-session mindfulness program reported significantly less burnout and occupational stress after intervention and at three-month follow-up than did those in the control group. Healthcare providers, including physicians, nurses, and psychologists, who participated in an eight-week mindfulness-based stress reduction course found significant improvements in well-being and burnout scores, as measured by the *Maslach Burnout Inventory*, including in the areas of Emotional Exhaustion ($p < 0.03$), Depersonalization ($p < 0.04$), and Personal Accomplishment ($p < 0.001$; Goodman & Schorling, 2012). Similarly, veterinary students who engaged in a mindfulness intervention evidenced increased well-being and decreased symptoms of depression and stress, both precursors to burnout (Drake et al., 2014). Sharp Donahoo et al. (2018) found teachers who practiced mindfulness more regularly had significantly lower scores in perceived stress over those who did not. In another randomized control study investigating mindfulness for teachers, results indicated those in the mindfulness training group to have significant reductions in psychological symptoms and burnout, whereas control group participants showed marginally significant increases in burnout symptoms (Flook et al., 2013). Mindfulness has also been shown to benefit intern doctors completing an emergency department rotation; a significantly greater reduction in burnout and stress was seen after participation in a ten-week mindfulness intervention when compared with the active control group (Ireland et al., 2017). Additionally, police officers who completed an eight-week mindfulness training program evidenced significant improvement in self-reported mindfulness, resilience, burnout, and mental and physical health, including fatigue and among other variables (Christopher et al., 2016). The AVMA (n.d.) also advocates for the use of mindfulness and meditation to decrease symptoms of stress and burnout. Overall, mindfulness has been evidenced to reduce burnout in the helping professions (Seney & Mishou, 2018).

In general, increasing psychological flexibility and mindfulness have been found to show promise for reducing burnout in a variety of professions, with research supporting its use. Both mindfulness and increasing psychological flexibility are key components in ACT.

Trauma-Related Employment Stress and ACT

TRES, including CF, STS, and VT, is another area wherein ACT has been found to be efficacious. This section reviews the components of ACT as they relate to TRES in the helping professions and caregiving.

Compassion Fatigue

Those who work in the helping professions are uniquely vulnerable to experience symptoms of CF. These professions are responsible for the well-being of others, such as the community, patients, clients, and animals that they serve. Because CF among providers can negatively affect the health and treatment outcomes of the recipient of the services, there is an ethical obligation for the provider to identify and implement strategies to prevent and remedy CF (Negash & Sahin, 2011). ACT has been found to be useful for those with CF.

Health providers, such as physicians, nurses, veterinarians, and mental health professionals, are at high risk for developing CF symptoms as compared with other professions. Psychological flexibility and mindfulness have been indicated as protective factors against CF. In a study of nurses, Duarte and Pinto-Gouveia (2017) discovered that nurses who are more prone to burnout and CF tended to have more psychological inflexibility than their peers. Taxing caregiving roles combined with little psychological flexibility appear to create a situation more prone to developing CF, with increased psychological flexibility helping to protect against these symptoms. In related research, 15 nurses were trained in the practice of mindfulness (breathing and meditation exercises) and measured on their current and postvention scores in a variety of well-being areas. The mindfulness intervention demonstrated a statistically significant increase in compassion satisfaction scores and decreases in burnout and STS scores. These positive results remained at six-month follow-up for those participants who responded (Hevezi, 2016). Mindfulness has also been found to be helpful in reducing CF symptoms with psychologists and social workers. In a sample of 77 clinical psychologists, the participants' level of mindfulness appeared to have preventive qualities against CF levels (Yip et al., 2017). In an exploratory study, interns in social work were rated on their mindfulness levels and their risk for CF. Results suggest that mindfulness positively correlates with greater potential for compassion satisfaction ($r = 0.46$, $p < 0.00$) while lower levels of mindfulness increased a student's risk for CF ($r = -0.53$, $p < 0.00$), suggesting that mindfulness may be a protective factor for those in helping professions (Decker et al., 2015).

ACT has also been studied with partners of cancer patients (Köhle et al., 2015) and parents of children diagnosed with major medical conditions, such as cerebral palsy (Whittingham et al., 2016) and autism (Poddar et al., 2015), with results finding treatment improvements in the areas of caregiver state anxiety, depression, and psychological flexibility. Other studies have found similar results, with a two-day ACT parent workshop improving parent mental health and reducing CF. Results from other studies on ACT concur with these findings (Brown et al., 2014).

The existing evidence suggests that ACT may have promise in helping caregivers adjust to the difficulties in their role and buffering against CF. As in burnout, increasing psychological flexibility and mindfulness appear to be key mechanisms in the ACT framework.

Vicarious Trauma and Secondary Traumatic Stress

VT and STS are more common among the helping professions, wherein professionals and caregivers are exposed to clients (people or animals) who have been traumatized themselves. The helping professions most at-risk for VT and STS are social workers (Bride, 2007); child protective service workers (Bride et al., 2007); military personnel (Lautieri, 2020); military health providers (Cieslak et al., 2013); police officers, firefighters, and first responders (Lautieri, 2020); veterinarians (AVMA, n.d.); and general trauma therapists (Elwood et al., 2011). ACT has been found to have merit when addressing trauma among those in these caregiving roles.

Prior research supports ACT as an effective intervention for those who have symptoms of post-traumatic stress disorder (PTSD; Orsillo & Batten, 2005; Pohar & Argáez, 2017). PTSD can be conceptualized in part as a disorder maintained in the traumatized individual via excessive, ineffective attempts to control unwanted memories, thoughts, and feelings. This attempt to try and control or avoid thoughts has been found to paradoxically maintain or increase the frequency of the unwanted experiences (Hayes et al., 1996; Kumpula et al., 2011). Therefore, it is theorized that ACT can be a powerful intervention due to the fostering of acceptance within the individual wherein experiential avoidance is reduced (Orsillo & Batten, 2005). Research supports ACT's effectiveness in targeting avoidance behavior and as a form of exposure therapy, which is arguably one of the most effective interventions for PTSD (Thompson et al., 2013). Additionally, acceptance or tolerance of distress may be more important in facilitating new learning than simply habituation to feared stimuli, such as that in exposure therapy (e.g., Craske et al., 2008; Kircanski et al., 2012). In addition to being helpful in the treatment of PTSD, the same processes in ACT are thought to hold value for those suffering from VT and STS.

In a study examining STS in foster caregivers, avoidant cognitive styles of psychological inflexibility and thought suppression were associated with higher levels of STS. Results indicated that 19.8% of participants were at-risk for STS while 25.2% presented as high risk for STS. Psychological inflexibility was significantly and positively correlated to STS ($r = 0.349$, $p < 0.001$) in this sample. Clinical implications of this study, according to the authors, included increasing caregiver well-being through reflective practice and clinical interventions targeting inflexible cognitive styles, such as ACT and mindfulness (Hannah & Woolgar, 2018). Nurses also have been found to have high levels of STS symptoms. Dominguez-Gomez and Rutledge's (2009) research involving emergency department nurses found that 54% of their sample had arousal symptoms, such as irritability, followed by avoidance symptoms (52%), and intrusion symptoms (intrusive thoughts at 46%). The majority of nurses (85%) reported at least one symptom in the past week, with 33% reporting all symptoms. Other studies have found similar outcomes, with almost half of the sample of nurses meeting criteria for STS (Ratrout & Hamdan-Mansour, 2020). Similarly, high levels have been reported among detective officers investigating child protection cases with 51% of respondents reported some degree of STS symptomatology, 40% reported mild to moderate symptoms, and 11% reported high or severe symptoms, as measured by the Secondary Traumatic Stress Scale (STSS; MacEachern et al., 2019). ACT's primary mechanisms are to reduce avoidance and increase acceptance and psychological flexibility, thereby likely buffering against the symptoms of STS, though more research is needed in this area.

Parents can also experience trauma-related symptoms through caregiving, of which ACT can be a helpful intervention. Burke et al. (2014) piloted an ACT intervention with parents of children previously diagnosed with a life-threatening illness (cardiac problems and cancer). Parents completed pre-, post-, and six-month follow-up surveys assessing the emotional impact of the child's illness, parent posttraumatic stress, and psychological elements targeted by the intervention (mindfulness and flexibility). Significant reductions in parental post-traumatic stress and emotional impact from their child's illness were found postvention, along with significant improvements in parental mindfulness and psychological flexibility, with medium to large effect sizes found; these outcomes were maintained at 6 month follow-up.

Mindfulness has also been shown to be helpful in reducing VT and STS symptoms in the helping professions. In a sample of 71 mental health clinicians who work with trauma survivors, clinicians who had higher self-reported mindfulness qualities had significantly lower VT symptoms (Jacob & Holczer, 2016). Firefighters, who have been found to have high rates of VT through their employment, were studied to determine the role of mindfulness in their rates of developing VT and other related stress symptoms. Results from this sample found mindfulness negatively predicted all of the VT symptoms assessed. The researchers recommended that mindfulness be practiced by firefighters to help protect them against the stressors of their role (Setti & Argentero, 2014). Consistent with this, a study conducted by Harker et al. (2016) of 133 human service professionals working in the fields of psychology, social work, counseling, and youth and foster care work explored the predictive relationship between resilience, mindfulness, and psychological distress. Results evidenced that higher levels of resilience and mindfulness were a significant predictor of lower levels of psychological distress, burnout, and secondary traumatic stress. Here, too, the researchers recommend mindfulness practices be implemented in the human service professions to help prevent STS. Therefore, both the psychological flexibility and mindfulness components of ACT have been found to be powerful prevention and intervention tools for TRES in the helping professions.

Concluding Comments

Burnout and TRES in the helping professions have been well documented, with the helping roles leaving individuals at a higher vulnerability for these stress-related symptoms. ACT combines mindfulness and acceptance practices to move individuals toward values-based goals, all while increasing psychological flexibility. Given that the core precursors of burnout and TRES is a lack of psychological flexibility, along with restrictive, repetitive thinking and a lack of mindful awareness, ACT is well suited to both prevent and intervene in burnout and TRES. In the chapters that follow, we explore specific interventions associated with each of the components of ACT as they relate to intervention for these syndromes among helping professionals.

References

American Veterinary Medical Association. (n.d.). *Work and compassion fatigue.* https://www. avma.org/resources-tools/wellbeing/work-and-compassion-fatigue

Arch, J. J., Eifert, G. H., Davies, C., Vilardaga, J. C. P., Rose, R. D., & Craske, M. G. (2012). Randomized clinical trial of cognitive behavioral therapy (CBT) versus acceptance and commitment therapy (ACT) for mixed anxiety disorders. *Journal of Consulting and Clinical Psychology, 80*(5), 750–765. https://doi.org/10.1037/a0028310.

Biglan, A., Layton, G. L., Jones, L. B., Hankins, M., & Rusby, J. C. (2013). The value of workshops on psychological flexibility for early childhood special education staff. *Topics in Early Childhood Special Education, 32*(4), 196–210. https://doi.org/10.1177/0271121411425191.

Bluett, E. J., Homan, K. J., Morrison, K. L., Levin, M. E., & Twohig, M. P. (2014). Acceptance and commitment therapy for anxiety and OCD spectrum disorders: An empirical review. *Journal of Anxiety Disorders, 28*(6), 612–624. https://doi.org/10.1016/j.janxdis.2014.06.008.

Bride, B. E. (2007). Prevalence of secondary traumatic stress among social workers. *Social Work, 52*(1), 63–70. https://doi.org/10.1093/sw/52.1.63.

Bride, B. E., Jones, J. L., & Macmaster, S. A. (2007). Correlates of secondary traumatic stress in child protective services workers. *Journal of Evidenced Based Social Work, 4*(3–4), 69–80. https://doi.org/10.1300/J394v04n03_05.

Brinkborg, H., Michanek, J., Hesser, H., & Berglund, G. (2011). Acceptance and commitment therapy for the treatment of stress among social workers: A randomized controlled trial. *Behaviour Research and Therapy, 49*(6–7), 389–398. https://doi.org/10.1016/j.brat.2011.03.009.

Brown, K. W., Wittingham, K., Boyd, R. N., McKinlay, L., & Sofronoff, K. (2014). Improving child and parenting outcomes following pediatric acquired brain injury: A randomized controlled trial of stepping stones triple P plus acceptance and commitment therapy. *Journal of Child Psychology and Psychiatry, 55*(10), 1172–1183. https://doi.org/10.1111/jcpp.12227.

Burke, K., Muscara, F., McCarthy, M., Dimovski, A., Hearps, S., Anderson, V., & Walser, R. (2014). Adapting acceptance and commitment therapy for parents of children with life-threatening illness: Pilot study. *Families, Systems & Health, 32*(1), 122–127. https://doi.org/10.1037/fsh0000012.

Christopher, M. S., Goerling, R. J., Rogers, B. S., Hunsinger, M., Baron, G., Bergman, A. L., & Zava, D. T. (2016). A pilot study evaluating the effectiveness of a mindfulness-based intervention on cortisol awakening response and health outcomes among law enforcement officers. *Journal of Police and Criminal Psychology, 31*, 15–28. https://doi.org/10.1007/s11896-015-9161-x.

Cieslak, R., Anderson, V., Bock, J., Moore, B. A., Peterson, A. L., & Benight, C. C. (2013). Secondary traumatic stress among mental health providers working with the military: Prevalence and its work- and exposure-related correlates. *Journal of Nervous and Mental Disorders, 201*(11), 917–925. https://doi.org/10.1097/NMD.0000000000000034.

Craske, M. G., Kircanski, K., Zelikowsky, M., Mystkowski, J., Chowdhury, N., & Baker, A. (2008). Optimizing inhibitory learning during exposure therapy. *Behaviour Research and Therapy, 46*(1), 5–27. https://doi.org/10.1016/j.brat.2007.10.003.

Decker, T., Brown, J. L., Ong, J., & Stiney-Ziskind, C. A. (2015). Mindfulness, compassion fatigue, and compassion satisfaction among social work interns. *Social Work & Christianity, 42*(1), 28–41. https://www.nacsw.org/publications/journal-swc/.

Dominguez-Gomez, E., & Rutledge, D. N. (2009). Prevalence of secondary traumatic stress among emergency nurses. *Journal of Emergency Nursing, 35*(3), 199–274. https://doi.org/10.1016/j.jen.2008.05.003.

Donaldson, E., & Bond, F. W. (2004). Psychological acceptance and emotional intelligence in relation to workplace Well-being. *British Journal of Guidance and Counselling, 32*(2), 187–203. https://doi.org/10.1080/0806980041001692210.

Drake, A. S., Hafen, M., & Rush, B. R. (2014). Promoting Well-being among veterinary medical students: Protocol and preliminary findings. *Journal of Veterinary Medical Education, 41*(3), 294–300. https://doi.org/10.3138/jvme.0214-026R.

Duarte, J., & Pinto-Gouveia, J. (2017). The role of psychological factors in oncology nurses' burnout and compassion fatigue symptoms. *European Journal of Oncology Nursing, 28*, 114–121. https://doi.org/10.1016/j.ejon.2017.04.002.

Eilenberg, T., Finkl, P., Jensen, J. S., Rief, W., & Frostholm, L. (2016). Acceptance and commitment group therapy (ACT-G) for health anxiety: A randomized controlled trial. *Psychological Medicine, 46*(1), 103–105. https://doi.org/10.1017/S0033291715001579.

Elwood, L. S., Mott, J., Lohr, J. M., & Galovski, T. E. (2011). Secondary trauma symptoms in clinicians: A critical review of the construct, specificity, and implications for trauma-focused treatment. *Clinical Psychology Review, 31*(1), 25–36. https://doi.org/10.1016/j.cpr.2010.09.004.

Emerson, L. M., Leyland, A., Hudson, K., Rowse, G., Hanley, P., & Hugh-Jones, S. (2017). Teaching mindfulness to teachers: A systematic review and narrative synthesis. *Mindfulness, 8*(5), 1136–1149. https://doi.org/10.1007/s12671-017-0691-4.

Feros, D. L., Lane, L., Ciarrochi, J., & Blackledge, J. T. (2011). Acceptance and commitment therapy (ACT) for improving the lives of cancer patients: A preliminary study. *Psychooncology, 22*(2), 459–464. https://doi.org/10.1002/pon.2083.

Flook, L., Goldberg, S. B., Pinger, L., Bonus, K., & Davidson, R. J. (2013). Mindfulness for teachers: A pilot study to assess effects on stress, burnout and teaching efficacy. *Mind Brain Education, 7*(3), 186–195. https://doi.org/10.1111/mbe.12026.

Forman, E. M., Herbert, J. D., Moitra, E., Yeomans, P. D., & Geller, P. A. (2007). A randomized controlled effectiveness trial of acceptance and commitment therapy and cognitive therapy for anxiety and depression. *Behavior Modification, 31*(6), 772–799. https://doi.org/10.1177/0145445507302202.

Frank, J. L., Reibel, D., Broderick, P., Cantrell, T., & Metz, S. (2015). The effectiveness of mindfulness-based stress reduction on educator stress and well-being: Results from a pilot study. *Mindfulness, 6*, 208–216. https://doi.org/10.1007/s12671-013-0246-2.

Goodman, M. J., & Schorling, J. B. (2012). A mindfulness course decreases burnout and improves Well-being among healthcare providers. *The International Journal of Psychiatry in Medicine, 43*(2), 119–128. https://doi.org/10.2190/PM.43.2.b.

Greco, L. A., Blackledge, J. T., Coyne, L. W., & Enreheich, J. (2005). Integrating acceptance and mindfulness into treatments for child and adolescent anxiety disorders: Acceptance and commitment therapy as an example. In S. M. Orsillo & L. Roemer (Eds.), *Acceptance and mindfulness-based approaches to anxiety: Conceptualization and treatment* (pp. 301–322). Kluwer/Plenum.

Hancock, K., Swain, J., Hainsworth, C., Koo, S., & Dixon, A. (2016). Long term follow up in children with anxiety disorders treated with acceptance and commitment therapy or cognitive behavioral therapy: Outcomes and predictors. *Journal of Child and Adolescent Behavior, 4*(5), 317–330. https://doi.org/10.4172/2375-4494.1000317.

Hannah, B., & Woolgar, M. (2018). Secondary trauma and compassion fatigue in foster carers. *Clinical Child Psychology and Psychiatry, 23*(4), 629–643. https://doi.org/10.1177/1359104518778327.

Harker, R., Pidgeon, A. M., Klaassen, F., & King, S. (2016). Exploring resilience and mindfulness as preventative factors for psychological distress burnout and secondary traumatic stress among human service professionals. *Work, 54*(3), 631–637. https://doi.org/10.3233/WOR-162311.

Harris, R. (2009). *ACT made simple: A quick start guide to ACT basics and beyond.* New Harbinger.

Hayes, S. C. (2004). Acceptance and commitment therapy. In S. C. Hayes, V. M. Follette, & M. M. Linehan (Eds.), *Mindfulness and acceptance: Expanding the cognitive-behavioral tradition* (pp. 1–29). Guilford Press.

Hayes, S. C. (2005). *Get out of your mind and into your life: The new acceptance and commitment therapy.* New Harbinger.

Hayes, S. C., Wilson, K. G., Gifford, E. V., Follette, V. M., & Strosahl, K. (1996). Experiential avoidance and behavioral disorders: A functional dimensional approach to diagnosis and treatment. *Journal of Consulting and Clinical Psychology, 64*(6), 1152–1168. https://doi.org/10.1037/0022-006X.64.6.1152.

Hayes, S. C., Luoma, J. B., Bond, F. W., Masuda, A., & Lillis, J. (2006). Acceptance and commitment therapy: Model, processes and outcomes. *Behaviour Research and Therapy, 44*(1), 1–25. https://doi.org/10.1016/j.brat.2005.06.006.

Hayes, S. C., Strosahl, K. D., & Wilson, K. G. (2012). *Acceptance and commitment therapy: An experiential approach to behavior change* (2nd ed.). Guilford Press.

Hevezi, J. A. (2016). Evaluation of a meditation intervention to reduce the effects of stressors associated with compassion fatigue among nurses. *Journal of Holistic Nursing, 34*(4), 343–350. https://doi.org/10.1177/0898010115615981.

Hinds, E., Jones, L. B., Gau, J. M., Forrester, K. K., & Biglan, A. (2015). Teacher distress and the role of experiential avoidance. *Psychology in the Schools, 52*(3), 284–297. https://doi.org/10.1002/pits.21821.

Ireland, M. J., Clough, B., Gill, K., Langan, F., O'Connor, A., & Spencer, L. (2017). A randomized controlled trial of mindfulness to reduce stress and burnout among intern medical practitioners. *Medical Teacher, 39*(4), 409–414. https://doi.org/10.1080/0142159X.2017.1294749.

Jacob, C. J., & Holczer, R. (2016). The role of mindfulness in reducing trauma counselors' vicarious traumatization. *Journal of the Pennsylvania Counseling Association, 15*, 31–38. http://pacounseling.org/aws/PACA/asset_manager/get_file/129164?ver=44.

Jeffcoat, T., & Hayes, S. C. (2012). A randomized trial of ACT bibliotherapy on the mental health of K-12 teachers and staff. *Behaviour Research and Therapy, 50*(9), 571–579. https://doi.org/10.1016/j.brat.2012.05.008.

Jonsjö, M. A., Wicksell, R. K., Holmström, L., Andreasson, A., & Olsson, G. L. (2019). Acceptance & Commitment Therapy for ME/CFS (chronic fatigue syndrome) – A feasibility study. *Journal of Contextual Behavioral Science, 12*, 89–97. https://doi.org/10.1016/j.jcbs.2019.02.008.

Kerr, S. L., Lucas, L. J., DiDomenico, G. E., Mishra, V., Stanton, B. J., Shivde, G., Pero, A. N., Runyen, M. E., & Terry, G. M. (2017). Is mindfulness training useful for pre-service teachers? An exploratory investigation. *Teaching Education, 28*(4), 349–359. https://doi.org/10.1080/10476210.2017.1296831.

Kircanski, K., Mortazvi, A., Castriotta, N., Baker, A. S., Mystkowski, J. L., Yi, R., & Craske, M. G. (2012). Challenges to the traditional exposure paradigm: Variability in exposure therapy for contamination fears. *Journal of Behavior Therapy and Experimental Psychiatry, 43*(2), 745–751. https://doi.org/10.1016/j.jbtep.2011.10.010.

Köhle, N., Drossaert, C. H., Schreurs, K. M., Hagedoorn, M., Verdonck de Leeuw, I., & Bohlmeijer, E. T. (2015). A web-based self-help intervention for partners of cancer patients based on acceptance and commitment therapy: A protocol of a randomized controlled trial. *BMC Public Health, 15*(303), 1–13. https://doi.org/10.1186/s12889-015-1656-y.

Kumpula, M. J., Orcutt, H. K., Bardeen, J. R., & Varkovitzky, R. L. (2011). Peritraumatic dissociation and experiential avoidance as prospective predictors of posttraumatic stress symptoms. *Journal of Abnormal Psychology, 120*(3), 617–627. https://doi.org/10.1037/a0023927.

Lautieri, A. (2020). *7 high-risk professions that can lead to PTSD*. Desert Hope: American Addiction Centers. https://deserthopetreatment.com/co-occurring-disorders/ptsd/high-risk-professions/.

Lloyd, J., Bond, F. W., & Flaxman, P. E. (2013). The value of psychological flexibility: Examining psychological mechanisms underpinning a cognitive behavioural therapy intervention for burnout. *Work & Stress, 27*(2), 181–199. https://doi.org/10.1080/02678373.2013.782157.

MacEachern, A. D., Dennis, A. A., Jackson, S., & Jindal-Snape, D. (2019). Secondary traumatic stress: Prevalence and symptomology amongst detective officers investigating child protection cases. *Journal of Police and Criminal Psychology, 34*, 165–174. https://doi.org/10.1007/s11896-018-9277-x.

Maslach, C., & Leiter, M. P. (2016). Understanding the burnout experience: Recent research and its implications for psychiatry. *World Psychiatry, 15*(2), 103–111. https://doi.org/10.1002/wps.20311.

McCracken, L. M., & Vowles, K. E. (2014). Acceptance and commitment therapy and mindfulness for chronic pain: Model, process, and progress. *American Psychologist, 69*(2), 178–187. https://doi.org/10.1037/a0035623.

Najvani, B. D., Neshatdoosst, H. T., Abedi, M. R., & Mokarian, F. (2015). The effect of acceptance and commitment therapy on depression and psychological flexibility in women with breast cancer. *Zahedan Journal of Research in Medical Sciences, 17*(4), e965. https://www.sid.ir/en/journal/ViewPaper.aspx?id=468763.

Negash, S., & Sahin, S. (2011). Compassion fatigue in marriage and family therapy: Implications for therapists and clients. *Journal of Marital and Family Therapy, 37*(1), 1–13. https://doi.org/10.1111/j.1752-0606.2009.00147.x.

O'Brien, K. M., Larson, C. M., & Murrell, A. R. (2008). Third-wave behavior therapies for children and adolescents: Progress, challenges and future directions. In L. A. Greco & S. C. Hayes (Eds.), *Acceptance & mindfulness treatments for children and adolescents: A practitioner's guide* (pp. 15–35). New Harbinger.

Orsillo, S. M., & Batten, S. V. (2005). Acceptance and commitment therapy in the treatment of posttraumatic stress disorder. *Behavior Modification, 29*(1), 95–129. https://doi.org/10.1177/0145445504270876.

Poddar, S., Sinha, V. K., & Urbi, M. (2015). Acceptance and commitment therapy on parents of children and adolescents with autism spectrum disorders. *International Journal of Educational and Psychological Researches, 1*(3), 221–225. https://doi.org/10.4103/2395-2296.158331.

Pohar, R., & Argáez, C. (2017). *Acceptance and commitment therapy for post-traumatic stress disorder, anxiety, and depression: A review of clinical effectiveness*. Canadian Agency for Drugs and Technologies in Health. https://www.ncbi.nlm.nih.gov/books/NBK525684/.

Ratrout, H. F., & Hamdan-Mansour, A. M. (2020). Secondary traumatic stress among emergency nurses: Prevalence, predictors, and consequences. *International Journal of Nursing Practice, 26*(1), e12767–e12773. https://doi.org/10.1111/ijn.12767.

Roeser, R. W., Schonert-Reichl, K. A., Jha, A., Cullen, M., Wallace, L., Wilensky, R., Oberle, E., Thomson, K., Taylor, C., & Harrison, J. (2013). Mindfulness training and reductions in teacher stress and burnout: Results from two randomized, waitlist-control field trials. *Journal of Educational Psychology, 105*(3), 787–804. https://doi.org/10.1037/a0032093.

Scott, W., Hann, K. E. J., & McCracken, L. M. (2016). A comprehensive examination of changes in psychological flexibility following acceptance and commitment therapy for chronic pain. *Journal of Contemporary Psychotherapy, 46*(3), 139–148. https://doi.org/10.1007/s10879-016-9328-5.

Seney, R. W., & Mishou, M. A. (2018). The importance of mindfulness training for teachers. *Gifted Education International, 34*(2), 155–161. https://doi.org/10.1177/0261429417716349.

Setti, I., & Argentero, P. (2014). The role of mindfulness in protecting firefighters from psychosomatic malaise. *Traumatology: An International Journal, 20*(2), 134–141. https://doi.org/10.1037/h0099398.

Sharp Donahoo, L. M., Siegrist, B., & Garrett-Wright, D. (2018). Addressing compassion fatigue and stress of special education teachers and professional staff using mindfulness and prayer. *The Journal of School Nursing, 34*(6), 442–448. https://doi.org/10.1177/1059840517725789.

Thompson, B. L., Luoma, J. B., & LeJeune, J. T. (2013). Using acceptance and commitment therapy to guide exposure-based interventions for posttraumatic stress disorder. *Journal of Contemporary Psychotherapy, 43*(3), 133–140. https://doi.org/10.1007/s10879-013-9233-0.

Twohig, M. P., & Levin, M. E. (2017). Acceptance and commitment therapy as a treatment for anxiety and depression: A review. *Psychiatric Clinics of North America, 40*(4), 751–770. https://doi.org/10.1016/j.psc.2017.08.009.

Udell, C. J., Ruddy, J. L., & Procento, P. M. (2018). Effectiveness of acceptance and commitment therapy in increasing resilience and reducing attrition of injured US navy recruits. *Military Medicine, 183*(9/10), e603–e611. https://doi.org/10.1093/milmed/usx109.

Veehof, M. M., Trompetter, H. R., Bohlmeijer, E. T., & Schreurs, K. M. G. (2016). Acceptance- and mindfulness-based interventions for the treatment of chronic pain: A meta-analytic review. *Cognitive Behavior Therapy, 45*(1), 5–31. https://doi.org/10.1080/16506073.2015.1098724.

Whittingham, K., Sanders, M., McKinlay, L., & Boyd, R. (2016). Parenting intervention combined with acceptance and commitment therapy: A trial with families of children with cerebral palsy. *Journal of Pediatric Psychology, 41*(5), 531–542. https://doi.org/10.1093/jpepsy/jsv118.

Wicksell, R. K., Melin, L., & Olsson, G. L. (2007). Exposure and acceptance in the rehabilitation of adolescents with idiopathic chronic pain – A pilot study. *European Journal of Pain, 11*(3), 267–274. https://doi.org/10.1016/j.ejpain.2006.02.012.

Wicksell, R. K., Olsson, G. L., & Hayes, S. (2011). Psychological flexibility as a mediator of improvement in acceptance and commitment therapy for patients with chronic pain following whiplash. *European Journal of Pain, 14*(10), 1059e.1–1059e.11. https://doi.org/10.1016/j.ejpain.2010.05.001.

Yip, S. Y., Mak, W. W., Chio, F. H., & Law, R. W. (2017). The mediating role of self-compassion between mindfulness and compassion fatigue among therapists in Hong Kong. *Mindfulness, 8*(2), 460–470. https://doi.org/10.1007/s12671-016-0618-5.

Chapter 3
Mindfulness and Acceptance Practices

This chapter reviews mindfulness and acceptance practices, associated with acceptance and commitment therapy (ACT), as preventative measures and interventions for burnout and trauma-related employment stress (TRES). An overview of well-being as it relates to stress in the helping professions is discussed. Specific mindfulness and acceptance techniques, including practical tools, are offered.

Mindfulness Practices

Mindfulness practices have been mainstreamed for use with a variety of adult populations (Crane, 2017). From tech companies to hospitals, mindfulness has become a buzzword and a regular practice encouraged in the workplace. Burnout and TRES are common experiences for those working in the helping professions, including teachers, mental health professionals, physicians, veterinarians, first responders, and other caregivers. Mindfulness can address some of these burnout and TRES effects. This section reviews specific mindfulness techniques that are applicable to adults in the helping professions.

Psychoeducation on Stress and Well-Being

Before beginning any mindfulness-related practice, it is helpful to understand how our brains and bodies work when confronted with stress. Hanson and Mendius (2009) discuss the idea of "sticks" and "carrots" as they relate to our nervous system response and corresponding behavior. "Sticks" alert our brain's fear center (the amygdala) and the part of the nervous system that accelerates heart rate, raises blood pressure, and constricts blood vessels (the sympathetic nervous system

© The Author(s), under exclusive license to Springer Nature Switzerland AG 2022
M. L. Holland et al., *Burnout and Trauma Related Employment Stress*,
https://doi.org/10.1007/978-3-030-83492-0_3

[SNS]) to the presence of a threat. Both are crucial in triggering a fight/flight/freeze response to the perceived threat. Chemicals in our bodies such as cortisol, adrenaline, and epinephrine are released in our bloodstream to elicit this survival mechanism. When the SNS is activated, our heart rate increases, blood pressure increases, and large muscle groups tense, among other physical alterations important to surviving a physical threat. On the other hand, "carrots" are things that we desire and work toward. They are also fueled by natural chemicals in our bodies, such as the neurotransmitter dopamine, and neuromodulators, such as endorphins, oxytocin, and norepinephrine. When released, these chemicals generate pleasurable and positively reinforcing sensations. Receiving a compliment at work, having a flirtation reciprocated, or winning at a game all likely trigger this pleasure system, leading us to want to repeat behaviors.

As suggested by Hanson and Mendius (2009), the "sticks" have been more influential in our ability to survive as a species and, therefore, we have evolved to pay greater attention to unpleasant or negative experiences. This "negativity bias" overlooks good news, emphasizes bad news, and creates uncomfortable feeling states, such as anxiety and depression. As the human species initially evolved, this phenomenon was highly adaptive (Nesse et al., 2016). For example, our ancestors' awareness of twigs snapping that may have signaled nearby predators, or being inclined to quickly identify poisonous versus healthy berries, helped ensure survival. Arguably, without this negativity bias, the human species may not have survived. However, when this survival mechanism is placed within today's society, it might be argued that thoughts triggered by this negativity bias have become a "twig snapping" experience, setting off a nervous system threat response (even in the absence of an objective threat to our physical integrity; Smith, 2011).

The other challenge is that we often replace the carrots (i.e., our goals or things we desire) that are in front of us with different, bigger, or more satisfying carrots. Once that particular carrot, or goal, is attained, we often quickly replace it with another. For example, we may put off activities to support our well-being, such as exercising or seeing friends, until the weekend. However, once the weekend comes, the carrot is often replaced, and the aim to focus on well-being is delayed until the next weekend, our upcoming vacation, or even retirement! All the while, days, months, and even years may go by, all lived in less than full health or satisfaction. Therefore, we are always striving toward the next goal, unaware that we engage in the replacement trick (switching of the carrots) and never truly reach the desired result (i.e., full-health and life satisfaction), leaving us depleted. In the helping professions, this process can contribute to burnout and TRES, as depicted in our glass of water metaphor from Chap. 1 (Fig. 1.1).

Mindfulness-Based Strategies

Understanding the carrots and sticks and how our nervous systems work under stress can be reassuring, as burnout and TRES can be isolating experiences. Mindfulness can help to deactivate the stress response and help us to perceive things more clearly as a way for us to "refill our glass." A summary of mindfulness strategies covered in this chapter is found in Table 3.1.

Breath Work

Breath is often considered the foundation of mindfulness, with connection to breath aiding focused attention and experiential awareness (the essence of mindfulness). Breath work is almost always used, no matter what mindfulness or meditation strategy is being implemented. The breath plays a powerful role in our ability to calm the body and mind to be able to increase conscious awareness of the present moment. Breath has been identified as a key component in mitigating the relaxation response, including activating the parasympathetic nervous system (PNS) and decreasing activation in the fight, flight, freeze response, or SNS (Asmundson & Stein, 1994; Elliott, 2010). Rapid breathing, particularly through the nose with increased inhalation versus exhalation, while offering an advantage of greater recognition of fearful stimuli and heightened arousal and vigilance in times of threat, leads to the activation of the SNS and can foster anxiety, and even panic, in the individual (Zelano et al., 2016). Breath utilizing deep, controlled inhalations and exhalations can help to reduce anxious symptoms (Walker & Pacik, 2017). Through the use of mindful breath, we can emerge out of the thinking mind and come back into the present moment.

There are various practices associated with mindful breath work. The breath works included in this chapter are three of the most common practices: diaphragmatic breathing, 4x8 breathing, and alternate nostril breathing (A.N.B.).

Diaphragmatic Breathing

Diaphragmatic breathing is the starting point for anyone doing breath work. The diaphragm is a dome-shaped structure that separates the chest, including the heart and lungs, from the abdomen, including organs related to digestion. Breathing in through the diaphragm aids the lungs in fully expanding with air and breathing out allows the muscle fibers of the diaphragm to relax, which thereby aids the relaxation response. Although we may assume breathing primarily involves the chest muscles, breathing primarily with the lungs arouses the SNS. However, breathing through the diaphragm increases parasympathetic activity, thereby increasing the relaxation response (Elliott, 2010). Therefore, in the practice of mindfulness, meditation, and relaxation, diaphragmatic breathing is essential. Decreasing the number of breaths taken per minute is also associated with increased PNS activation. Studies support the fact that SNS activity reduces when subjects breathe slowly (Oneda et al., 2010; Zelano et al., 2016). In most mindful breathing techniques, slow and controlled diaphragmatic breaths are recommended.

Table 3.1 Summary of mindfulness-based strategies in this chapter

Strategies	Definitions	Target process/outcome
Diaphragmatic breathing	Breathing in through the diaphragm aids the lungs in fully expanding with air and breathing out allows the muscle fibers of the diaphragm to relax (aiding the relaxation response)	Aids in the relaxation response, slows sympathetic nervous system arousal, sets the foundation for meditation, yoga, and other mindfulness techniques
4x8 breathing	Breathing into the count of 4, breathing out to the count of 8. Elongated exhales are linked to the relaxation response	Aids in the relaxation response, slows sympathetic nervous system arousal, sets the foundation for meditation, yoga, and other mindfulness techniques
Alternate nostril breathing	Closing off one nostril at a time during inhalation and exhalation. Helpful in reducing sympathetic nervous system activation	Reduces sympathetic nervous system activation. More helpful in reducing blood pressure levels than other forms of breath work
Progressive muscle relaxation	Different muscle groups are systematically tightened and released, often coupled with deep breathing	Reduces physical tension and anxiety. Works well with anxiety, stress, or somatic complaints
Focused meditation	The practice of focused attention involves intentionally directing and maintaining attention toward a target	This basic mindfulness practice helps to settle and focus the mind on a specific target. Works well for any presenting concern wherein thoughts are problematic
Open awareness meditation	Remaining aware of our surroundings and observing things happening without getting caught up in thoughts or judgments	This basic mindfulness practice helps to settle and focus the mind on the present moment. Works well for any presenting concern wherein thoughts are problematic
Gratitude and heartfulness	The act of focusing on what we are grateful for, along with increasing our desire to bond and connect with others and the world (heartfulness) has been shown to be linked to positive emotional well-being	Increases focus on the positive, thereby increasing well-being
Yoga	Yoga incorporates fluid movements, resting poses, and mindful breathing	Uniting body and mind in mindful poses
Mindful senses activities	The practice of utilizing and bringing awareness to the five senses without judgment	A tangible practice geared toward increasing mindful awareness
Mindful walking	Mindful walking is a way to practice moving without a goal or intention	A tangible practice geared towards increasing mindful awareness
Mindful listening	Mindful listening is paying attention to sounds in your environment, moment by moment, without judgment	A tangible practice geared toward increasing mindful awareness
Mindful eating	Mindful eating is paying attention to food using all five senses, moment by moment, without judgment	A tangible practice geared toward increasing mindful awareness

4×8 Breathing

The 4×8 breathing practice is an easy to follow, prescriptive technique that most adults can pick up right away. To begin, get into a comfortable seated position and either soften your gaze or close your eyes. Then begin to take in deep breaths into the count of four through your nose, and out to the count of eight through your mouth. As you practice this skill, focus your attention on your breath, noticing any bodily sensations that may be occurring throughout (e.g., the temperature of the air as it enters/exits your nose and the rise and fall of your chest and stomach). This breathing technique can be one of focused meditation wherein you concentrate your attention on counting (e.g., "In, $1 - 2 - 3 - 4$, Out, $1 - 2 - 3 - 4 - 5 - 6 - 7 - 8$") to help interrupt any thoughts that may be going through your mind.

Alternate Nostril Breathing

The practice of alternate nostril breathing (A.N.B.) involves closing off one nostril at a time as we inhale and exhale. This technique has been found to be effective in reducing blood pressure (Telles et al., 2014) and nervous system activation (Sinha et al., 2013; Telles et al., 2014). A.N.B can be particularly helpful if we are having physiological symptoms (e.g., accelerated heart rate and high blood pressure) associated with stress and anxiety.

The practice of A.N.B is relatively simple. Begin by sitting in a quiet posture, such as sitting in a chair or crossed legged on the floor. Bring your right hand up to the nose and fold the index and the middle fingers so that the right thumb can be used to close the right nostril and the index finger can be used to close the left nostril. Using the right thumb, softly close the right nostril and inhale as slowly as you can through the left nostril, then close it with your index finger. Pause briefly, then open and exhale slowly through the right nostril. With the right nostril open, inhale slowly, then close it with the thumb. Pause briefly, then exhale through the left nostril. Once your exhalation is complete, inhale through the left. Pause before moving to the right. Repeat this pattern five to ten times.

Progressive Muscle Relaxation

Progressive muscle relaxation is a technique wherein different muscle groups are systematically tightened and released, often coupled with deep breathing. When we become anxious or stressed, our muscles often tighten, which can lead to physical ailments such as tightness in our shoulder, headaches, stomachaches, and the like. The theory behind progressive muscle relaxation is that if you create tension in a muscle, then release that tension, the muscle naturally relaxes (Holland et al., 2017). A sample of recommended poses you can follow is offered in Table 3.2.

Table 3.2 Sample progressive muscle relaxation poses

Before beginning the technique, you should be comfortably sitting in a chair, with feet firmly on the ground and using 4x8 breaths to help initially relax.
1. *Feet*: Curl your toes tightly and hold for 8–10 s before releasing.
2. *Legs*: Lift your legs slightly off the ground and point your toes up and back toward your shins. Hold for 8–10 s and relax.
3. *Thighs*: Press your knees together and hold them tightly, as if you are squishing something in between your knees. Hold for 8–10 s, and release.
4. *Stomach*: Tighten your stomach muscles and hold for 8–10 s, then release.
5. *Hands*: Curl your fingers and make two tight fists, holding for 8–10 s, and release.
6. *Arms/chest*: Press the palms of your hands together, like a praying position, with your hands over mid-chest. Hold it for 8–10 s, and release.
7. *Shoulders*: Lift your shoulders up, as if you are going to try and reach your ears. Hold this position for 8–10 s, and release.
8. *Face*: Scrunch/tighten up your facial muscles, including your cheeks, mouth, and nose muscles, and the muscles of your forehead. Hold for 8–10 s, then let go. End with 4x8 breaths.

Focused Meditation

The practice of focused attention helps to teach us how to settle our thinking minds. When we ruminate on our thoughts, we become distracted and mindless, often leading to unproductive, negative emotional states. Meditation, however, allows us to focus our attention, which helps to decrease ruminative thinking. The target for focused attention can either be external (e.g., an object in the room) or internal (e.g., breath or a part of our body).

Meditations and mantras can be a very powerful tool for the helper in their mindfulness practices. Focused attention meditation involves intentionally directing and maintaining attention toward a target, while open awareness meditation requires awareness of one's surroundings and observing things happening; both meditation practices reinforce living in the present moment without getting caught up in thoughts or judgments. Mantras, a form of an internal focused meditation, are also explored. Practical examples of specific meditations and mantras are offered below.

External Meditation An external object used for focused meditation is best if it is stable and consistent. Objects that are not stable, such as a television screen or people walking about, can be too distracting to create a situation most suitable for focused attention. Examples of objects to focus on externally could include (a) a candle, watching the flame; a sound, listening to a repetitive sound, such as a gong; and (c) a plant or other object, fixing your gaze on the item. An example of how an external object (a lit candle) can be used in meditation is outlined in the script provided in Table 3.3.

Internal Meditation As opposed to external meditation, wherein you are focusing on something outside of yourself, internal meditation shifts the focus inward. There are many ways to create a sense of internal focused attention. Various examples include (a) breath, noticing the rise and fall of your diaphragm; (b) visualization,

Table 3.3 Sample focused meditation script

1. Begin with some deep, diaphragmatic breaths. Start by sitting up in your chair, with your feet flat on the floor and your hands in your lap.
2. Now focus on relaxing your face as you breathe through your nose, into the count of four, hold the breath for 1 s, and then breathe out slowly to the count of eight. With each breath in and out, notice how your cheeks soften, and your jaw and forehead relax.
3. Now, as you are taking your deep, 4 x 8 breaths, put your attention on the candle in front of you. Notice how the colors are different at the top of the flame than the bottom. Notice how the flame flickers, almost like it is dancing. When a thought comes into your mind, just allow that thought to float away, just as easily as it came in, and turn your attention back onto your breathing and the flickering flame.
4. Take in one more deep breath in, and out and slowly return your awareness back into the room.

picturing a peaceful image or setting in your mind; (c) a mantra, repeating a grounding word, phrase, or sound in your mind; and (d) part of the body, focusing on a particular sensation or area of your body (feet, scalp). Any of the above can assist someone in the practice of internal meditation. In the next section, simple mantras will be more fully explored with examples of how mantras can be paired with internal meditation.

Simple Mantras Mantras are sounds or statements that can be repeated to assist in internal meditation. Common within many mantras is acknowledgment of the challenge or painful circumstance, identifying commonality or shared humanity around the experience, then completing with a compassionate statement (Ackerman, 2017). The following is an example of a mantra offered to assist us during times of suffering: (a) "This is suffering" (whatever you are experiencing that is painful); (b) "Suffering is part of being human" (acknowledge that all humans struggle and suffer); and (c) "May I care about and support myself" (a self-compassionate phrase). Begin this practice by silently repeating this mantra in your mind, paired with deep breathing. An example of how a mantra, coupled with breath, can be used in internal meditation is outlined in the script provided in Table 3.4. Regularly engaging in this form of breath work will help you become more focused, more aware of thoughts that enter your mind, and more relaxed to begin to work toward other forms of mindfulness, including open awareness meditation (which we will explore next). Note in this script you can either close your eyes or soften your gaze. This is important as sometimes, particularly if we have experienced trauma, we may not be comfortable with, or could be activated by, closing our eyes completely. Therefore, you have the option to lower your gaze in a non-focused manner.

Open Awareness Meditation

Open awareness meditation is one of the basic core skill sets in becoming more mindful of our internal and external worlds. As opposed to focused meditation, open awareness allows attention to our surroundings and observation of things happening

Table 3.4 Sample mantra (and breath) script

1. Begin with some deep, diaphragmatic breaths. Start by sitting up in your chair, with your feet flat on the floor and your hands in your lap. Imagine your spine is held by a thread coming from the top of your head and attached to the ceiling.

2. Now focus on relaxing your face as you breathe through your nose, into the count of four, hold the breath for 1 s, and then breathe out slowly to the count of eight. With each breath in and out, notice how your cheeks soften, and your jaw and forehead relax.

3. If you become distracted by something else in the room, or if your mind wanders, bring your attention back to your breath once you realize you have lost focus. Notice how your stomach rises and falls with each deep breath in and out.

4. You may notice that your breath is cool when you breathe in through your nostrils but warmer when you breath out through your nostrils. Now take in a deep breath in your nose, but this next breath out, breathe out through your mouth. Take deep breaths in through your nose to the count of four, and out through your mouth to the count of eight.

5. With this next breath, imagine you are breathing in the mantra, "In this moment, I am safe." Imagine that thought circulating through you as you breathe in. With the breath out, imagine breathing out the mantra, "In this moment, I am calm." Imagine that thought rooting and grounding you into this present moment.

6. Continue this cycle about four to six times, repeating the mantras coupled with your breath.

7. Slowly open your eyes and return our awareness back into the room.

Table 3.5 Open awareness meditation script

Begin with some deep, diaphragmatic breaths. Start by sitting up in your chair, with your feet flat on the floor and your hands in your lap. Imagine your spine is held by a thread coming from the top of your head and attached to the ceiling. Now, imagine you are in a boat out at sea. Your thoughts, feelings, and emotions are represented by the waves ebbing against the boat. As thoughts and feelings become more difficult, the emotional storm intensifies, and you may find it challenging to navigate the waves. Now, visualize your breath as an anchor to the present moment. The waves may continue to crash, but the anchor of your breath provides you with the grounding you need to ride out the emotional storm. Continue to use your deep diaphragmatic breaths until you notice the waters begin to calm.

around us without getting caught up in thoughts or judgments. The metaphor of breath as an anchor can also be useful (Germer, 2009). This is where we imagine we are the boat, our thoughts are the waves, and our breath is the anchor. When thoughts pull us in various directions "out to sea," we can use the breath to anchor us back mindfully to the present moment. An example of an open awareness meditation script is provided in Table 3.5.

Yoga

Yoga-based practices have been found to be helpful across a variety of helping professions. Yoga has been shown to increase teachers' positive affect, distress tolerance, and improve physical well-being, such as decreasing blood pressure and cortisol response; yoga has also been found to reduce stress and burnout for school-based employees (Harris et al., 2016; Nosaka & Okamura, 2015). Yoga has also been found to reduce burnout and improve self-care among nurses. In a pilot-level clinical trial, yoga participants reported significantly less emotional exhaustion and depersonalization as well as significantly higher self-care compared with controls after an eight-week yoga intervention (Alexander et al., 2015).

Yoga exercises, which incorporate fluid movements, resting poses, and mindful breathing, have become increasingly popular, and guided yoga flows for all levels are easily accessible through Internet searches. The following figures offer yoga postures and provide a starting off point for those new to yoga practices (Figs. 3.1, 3.2, 3.3, 3.4, 3.5, 3.6, 3.7 and 3.8).

Yoga at a Desk When at work and confined to a smaller space or sitting in a chair, you can also engage in various stretching and yoga poses. The following figures offer a few adaptations that you can try (Figs. 3.9, 3.10, 3.11, 3.12, 3.13 and 3.14).

Fig. 3.1 Child's pose
Notice where the point in
your body where your
breath feels the stro**ngest**

Fig. 3.2 Mountain pose
Stand with your feet
slightly apart, arms at your
side. Feel rooted to the
ground

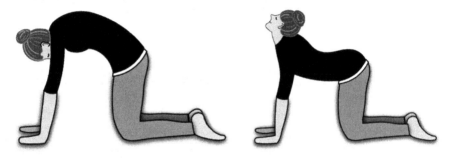

Fig. 3.3 Cat-cow pose
Tie your breath to your movement as you transition between **the poses**

Fig. 3.4 Forward
fold pose
As you breathe into this
fold, notice the lengthening
in your spine and **neck**

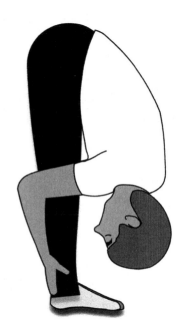

Mindful Senses (Walking, Listening, and Eating)

We can use our senses in a variety of ways to practice being mindful. There are several ways to use our senses: walking, listening, and eating. Mindful walking is moving without a goal or intention and is a tangible practice that cultivates mindful awareness. We often find ourselves walking from one place to the next ruminating on our agendas, plans, or past events. Mindful walking is a way to bring awareness back to the present moment through our senses and movement. As you walk, bring attention to your surroundings. Notice things you see in your environment, name

Fig. 3.5 Downward dog
Feel the stretch throughout **your body**

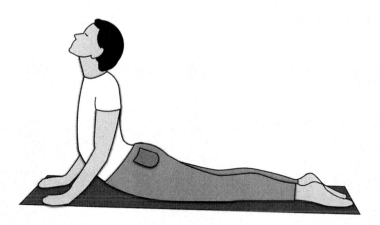

Fig. 3.6 Cobra pose
Notice the firing of your back and arm muscles as you breathe into yo**ur chest**

Fig. 3.7 Happy baby pose
As you breathe, notice your
spine against the floor and
your hips opening

Fig. 3.8 Corpse (Savasana) pose
Bring attention to your hands and feet as they rest against the floor; let your breath release any
tension you may be holding

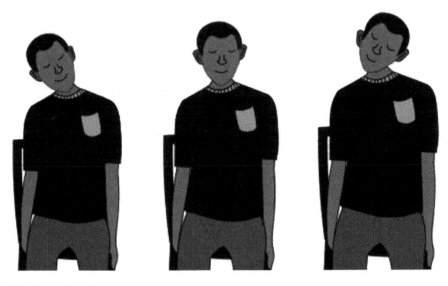

Fig. 3.9 Neck rolls

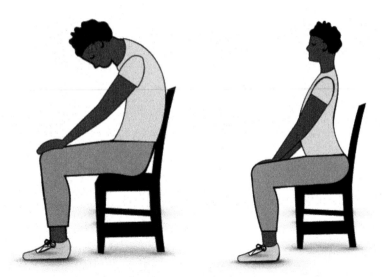

Fig. 3.10 Seated cat/cow

Fig. 3.11 Seated
forward bend

Fig. 3.12 Seated Twist

Fig. 3.13 Seated eagle

Fig. 3.14 Standing pigeon

the sounds you hear (birds, traffic, and our own footsteps/breathing), acknowledge smells and tastes, and bring attention to feelings/sensations (rhythm of your stride, air temperature, and feeling of your clothing/shoes). If you notice your mind wandering, bring your thoughts back to the sensation of walking without judgment.

Mindful listening is focusing your awareness on the sounds within the environment without judgment. The volume of our thoughts often drowns out the sounds in our environment and can draw our attention away from the world around us. When we do notice certain sounds, we can become annoyed or frustrated and view them as distractors. However, when we do not attach judgment to the sound, we are able to bring our awareness to the present moment. An example of a mindful listening script is provided in Table 3.6.

Another tangible mindfulness-based practice is mindful eating. Mindful eating is paying attention to our food using all five senses, moment by moment, without judgment. This practice enables appreciation for our food in each bite and brings attention more fully to our experience.

Mindful eating can be practiced with any food or drink, but to illustrate, we will describe the process using a chocolate candy, as shown in the script offered in Table 3.7. To follow along, we recommend getting a foil wrapped chocolate, or like food. Notice the candy using all five senses as if you were a visitor from another planet and had never encountered such objects before.

Table 3.6 Mindful listening script

Sit or stand wherever you are, at your desk, on the couch, on the train, etc. soften your gaze and bring your attention to the sounds around you in your environment. Notice the hum of the refrigerator, a car passing by outside, the muffled voices of family or friends in the next room, or the rustling of leaves blowing outside your window. Let what you hear connect you to the present moment. Invite yourself to notice sounds without judgment. Just listen. If you become restless, take notice and gently bring your attention back to the sounds around you.

Table 3.7 Mindful eating script

1. Start by picking up the object and noticing its appearance. Is it shiny or dull, bumpy or smooth?

2. What does the weight of it feel like in your hand? Does light catch the object differently in some places than others as you rotate it between your thumb and fingers?

3. Next, slowly unwrap the object. Do you notice any sounds as you do this?

4. Lift the object to your nose and bring your awareness to its scent. Breathe in deeply several times as you hold the object under your nose. What do you notice?

5. Next, place the object on your tongue. Very slowly bite down. What do you notice about the texture? Does it change? As you slowly chew the object, notice the flavor and consistency of it. Notice if you have any taste of the object left in your mouth after you have swallowed.

6. Consider how this experience differs from previous times you have eaten candy.

Acceptance Practices

In addition to mindfulness intervention, acceptance practices have been shown to help reduce stress and improve wellness and self-efficacy. Acceptance incorporates the ability to notice and experience all thoughts and feelings as they occur organically, without trying to reduce or eliminate any unpleasant thoughts and feelings, or to replace them with alternatives. When best understanding acceptance, it is helpful to first acknowledge the futility of avoidance. Experiential avoidance, or the tendency to avoid painful or challenging thoughts, feelings, and other internal experiences, is a common symptom of burnout. Eckhart Tolle (1999) notes that which we resist, persists. When we avoid issues or challenges, they tend to become more pronounced or lead to other problems. Therefore, acknowledging and addressing challenges and issues, as opposed to avoiding or ignoring these problems, is important. Of note is that acceptance is not the same thing as agreeing with or consenting. It is no longer avoiding the challenge and, instead, having a willingness to acknowledge the challenge and then choose what to do next. Without this acknowledgement, one becomes stuck in experiential avoidance (McCurry, 2009).

Acceptance of challenging situations has been found to increase psychological flexibility and decrease experiential avoidance, stress, and burnout in those who work in education (Hinds et al., 2015) and other helping professions, such as nurses, social workers, and substance abuse counselors (Brinkborg et al., 2011; Duarte & Pinto-Gouveia, 2017; Hayes et al., 2004). This idea has been validated through various research studies (Brinkborg et al., 2011; Lloyd et al., 2013). A key finding across studies is that ACT increases psychological flexibility, which can aid in

Table 3.8 Summary of acceptance-based strategies in this chapter

Strategies	Definitions
Clipboard technique	Using a solid object (e.g., a clipboard) to illustrate struggles with thoughts, feelings, behaviors, and situations and the difference between being flooded by them and simply noticing them
Chinese finger trap	Working with or visualizing a Chinese finger trap to represent challenges (difficult thoughts, feelings, memories, etc.) and understanding that when you lean into something uncomfortable, it gives you more space for acceptance and ability to respond to the challenge
Tug-of-war	Using the game tug-of-war as a metaphor helps to illustrate that attempting to control challenges is the problem. "Dropping the rope" frees you to experience challenges with more freedom and flexibility
Eating a piece of fruit	Utilizing the metaphor of eating a piece of fruit to illustrate the acceptance of an experience for what it is (i.e., a fruit) rather than comparing it to something else (i.e., a cookie)
"And"	Increasing the ability to have well-being in the midst of challenge by replacing the word "but" with "and"

decreased experiential avoidance and higher levels of acceptance of circumstances and effectiveness in participants' jobs (Biglan et al., 2013).

Various metaphors have been developed in ACT to assist with this process (Hayes et al., 2012). Simple examples that highlight the futility of "the struggle" (e.g., experiential avoidance) may include getting caught in quicksand, playing tug-of-war, or having one's fingers stuck in a Chinese finger trap. Each of these metaphors highlight that the more an individual struggles in these situations, the worse it becomes (Holland et al., 2017). The use of acceptance techniques can be utilized to help reduce experiential avoidance and fusion with thoughts (key ingredients in burnout), thereby increasing acceptance. Increasing mindful awareness and acceptance of the situation, including your own emotional experience, can assist in reducing reactivity and stress. Table 3.8 offers examples of popular metaphors and activities utilized in ACT and discussed in this section.

Clipboard Technique

There are many variations on this technique; typically, it involves a practitioner (e.g., therapist/counselor) working with a client using a solid object, such as a clipboard, as a metaphor for the thoughts, feelings, behaviors, or situations with which they are struggling (Harris, 2009). The clipboard metaphor can be referred to whenever you note you are feeling flooded by your challenges, or if you are trying to distract yourself or push these experiences and feelings away. Table 3.9 offers guided practice for this technique. This is written as if it was an exchange between a therapist and a client, but you can follow along with a solid object (e.g., a book and a piece of paper) as you read the script. We have found it helpful for some clients to bring the physicalized object with them into stressful situations as a reminder to set them down so that they can turn their attention toward the rest of the room. For example, if you are going into a stressful meeting, you can bring a clipboard into the meeting with you and hold it on your lap as a tangible reminder to work on your attachment toward the situation.

Table 3.9 Sample clipboard technique script

Therapist:	*Today we are going to do something a little different with the challenges you have been faced with. We will use a solid object as a metaphor. For our example, we will use a clipboard. I want you to imagine that this clipboard you are holding represents all of your challenges, including the difficult thoughts, feelings, and memories you have been struggling with. I would like you to take it in your hands and grip it as tightly as you can so that someone would not be able to pull it away from you.*
Client:	(grips it tightly)
Therapist:	*Good, now I would like you to bring it up close to your face where it is almost touching your nose. Now, how easy do you think it would be to continue our conversation with you gripping that so tightly?*
Client:	*Not very easy.*
Therapist:	*Would you imagine over time you might start to feel distracted or tired gripping that so tightly?*
Client:	(laughs) *Absolutely. I already am!*
Therapist:	*And what is your view of the room like as you are holding onto this so tight?*
Client:	*I can't see anything but the clipboard.*
Therapist:	*It can be hard to be so absorbed by our challenges and still be able to see clearly what is going on around you. How easy right now would it be to do the things that you love to do, such as typing on your computer or petting your cat?*
Client:	*Impossible!*
Therapist:	*Yes, it may be pretty difficult! When we are caught up in our challenges, it can be pretty impossible to see or do anything else. OK, you can release the clipboard now. OK, let's try something different. The clipboard still represents the challenges you have been struggling with. I want you to press your hands on one side of the clipboard, and I will press my hands on the other side, so we end up in a motion of pushing the clipboard back and forth.* (therapist sits closer to the client and begins the pushing movement with the clipboard once the client has pressed their hands on the other side of the board).
Therapist:	*Now, how easy would it be for us to continue our conversation?*
Client:	*Not easy at all, I am pretty distracted!*
Therapist:	*Do you imagine over time you would start to feel pretty fatigued?*
Client:	*Over time? I feel tired now!*
Therapist:	*How easy would it be for you to do the things you enjoy doing, like typing on your computer or petting your cat?*
Client:	*I would not be able to do those things. I'm too busy with this clipboard!*
Therapist:	*OK, good. Now go ahead and set the clipboard in your lap. Do you notice that it is still there?*
Client:	(sets clipboard loosely on their lap). *Yes.*
Therapist:	*Sure, you notice it is still there, but I am guessing there is a lot less effort devoted to it, perhaps you can see around the room a bit more clearly. How easy would it be now to have a conversation with me?*
Client:	*Very easy.*
Therapist:	*How easy would it be for you to do the things you enjoy doing?*
Client:	(mimes petting an imaginary cat next to them). *Yes, I could do those things.*
Therapist:	*So, no longer is the challenge you are having the only thing you can see* (therapist mimes putting the clipboard in front of their own face), *and no longer are you trying to push the thoughts and feelings away* (therapist mimes the pushing motion of the clipboard). *Instead, you notice that the challenge and those thoughts and feelings are still there, but you are devoting less energy towards them, just noticing them without attaching to them. This helps you see things around you more clearly and gives you more energy to do the things you love to do.*

The Chinese Finger Trap

The Chinese finger trap (a picture of a finger trap is offered in Fig. 3.15) metaphor is another tool to demonstrate acceptance of challenges and difficult thoughts, feelings, and emotions. The metaphor is discussed in the script below, as if it was a discussion between a client and a therapist (Table 3.10).

Fig. 3.15 Image of a Chinese finger trap

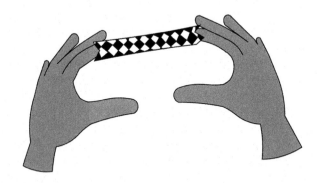

Table 3.10 Sample of Chinese finger trap script

Therapist:	*Today we are going to do something that helps demonstrate possible approaches to your challenges. This Chinese finger trap represents all of your challenges, including the difficult thoughts, feelings, and memories you have been struggling with. I would like you to take it in your hands and put your index fingers into the openings.*
Client:	(puts fingers into the toy).
Therapist:	*Good, now I would like you to pull your fingers apart from each other as if you're trying to escape the trap. What do you notice happening as you struggle to get your fingers out?*
Client:	*It's really latched onto my fingers!*
Therapist:	*That's right, it tightens. Do you feel more or less stuck as you try and pull your fingers out?*
Client:	*More, for sure.*
Therapist:	*Yes, pulling away from our challenges or trying to escape/avoid them can often make us feel more stuck. As we struggle against the discomfort, we find ourselves feeling trapped like our fingers in this finger trap. Now move your fingers slowly towards each other and relax. What do you notice?*
Client:	*It loosens up.*
Therapist:	*Yes, when we lean in and move towards the uncomfortable thoughts, feelings, and memories we find that their grip on our life can be loosened. Facing our challenges instead of struggling against them gives us more energy and we can see our problems more clearly when we are not actively trying to get out of the discomfort.*

Tug-of-War

The tug-of-war is another metaphor that helps to illustrate the challenge of attempting to control our difficult thoughts, feelings, behaviors, or situations as opposed to having acceptance around our current circumstances (Hayes et al., 2012). Table 3.11 offers a script for you to consider using this metaphor.

Eating a Piece of Fruit

Acceptance can be like eating a piece of fruit instead of a cookie. One reason for eating fruit could be that you are trying to eat healthier. Instead of your usual snack of a cookie, you eat a piece of fruit. You may "choose" fruit, but what will it be like to eat it? As you eat it, you start comparing it with the cookie. With each bite, you are thinking about how the fruit is not as sweet and crunchy as the cookie. Then, when you are done eating the fruit, you eat the cookie anyway. Another way to experience eating the fruit is to let the fruit be fruit, rather than needing or wanting it to be something it is not. You could notice the crunch of each bite, the juiciness, and the healthiness for what it is and not for what it is not, a cookie.

"And"

We often use the word "but," which invalidates our ability to have well-being in the midst of challenge. For example, we may say, "I want to feel better, but I have a lot of stress at work." The "but" negates the possibility of experiencing health in a time

Table 3.11 Sample of tug-of-war script

1. Imagine a monster made up of a challenge you are facing (anxiety, uncomfortable thoughts, feelings, memories, etc.). The monster is holding one end of a rope and you are holding the other end. In between is a deep seemingly bottomless pit. If you lose this game of tug-of-war, you would fall into the pit.
2. What are you going to do with this monster on the other end of the rope? Pull as hard as you can, right? Imagine what that might look like. As you pull, the monster pulls back. What might it feel like when your challenging thoughts, emotions, memories, and experiences pull back? Your challenges may intensify, get stronger, or seem more intimidating.
3. The tug-of-war battle doesn't stop between you and the monster. Sometimes it looks like you are winning when the challenges subside for a while. Other times the monster is winning, and you feel you are getting closer to the pit, but neither of you actually ever wins. You both just continue to tug back and forth. How frustrating and exhausting is this?
4. Where is your attention and effort focused? On your challenges or on the rest of life? As you pull, are you able to focus on and do things important to you? It does not seem likely.
5. Now imagine dropping the rope. The monster is still there, but you are no longer spending your focus and energy struggling against it. How do you imagine you would feel if you stopped pulling? You may find yourself less stuck and free to do the things that are important to you. And have more choice in how you respond to discomfort, pain, and challenges.

of challenge. The use of the word "and" means you can have the pain, challenge, and discomfort of your experience AND still work toward having greater well-being. Therefore, the thought would be replaced with "I want to feel better AND I have a lot of stress at work." This then allows for acceptance of the stress instead of giving up or giving into the stress, giving us the option to find ways of supporting ourselves during stressful times.

Case Examples

Derek

Derek, a 45-year-old police officer, noticed he was having trouble relaxing after he got off work. He began to have frequent awakenings during sleep, punctuated most nights with nightmares along the theme of threatened safety. Derek noticed a great deal of muscle tension in his shoulders and back. He became more moody and irritable, and began to isolate himself from family and friends. As he was driving with his partner on the job, his partner noticed that when the dispatcher would contact them on their radio, Derek would easily startle, seemingly jumpy and hypervigilant. His partner began to worry about him, and one night after work spoke with Derek about his concerns, offering to Derek that he may have symptoms of TRES. Derek, though initially resistant to the idea, began to research TRES and realized that, in fact, he was experiencing many of the symptoms. Derek decided to work with a master's level therapist to explore treatments for his condition.

The therapist met with Derek and confirmed that he was having symptoms consistent with TRES. Through their initial discussions, Derek confided in the therapist about various instances in which he was exposed to civilians' traumatic events. Derek shared that he began to frequently relive events that involved children in distress and often replayed them in his memory after work. The therapist recommended they utilize ACT approaches to address Derek's symptoms of TRES.

The therapist began the therapeutic work with a focus on mindfulness. The therapist explained to Derek how his repetitive thoughts focused on several of his high-intensity cases were causing him to experience significant activation of his sympathetic nervous system, even when not at work. These symptoms were interfering with his sleep and general well-being. Focusing first on mindful breath, Derek learned how to incorporate 4x8 breathing throughout the day to help bring down his nervous system reactivity. The therapist used this breathing technique and combined it with progressive muscle relaxation to assist Derek with his muscle tension. The therapist also used focused meditation with Derek, incorporating the mantra of, "In this moment I am calm," on the in-breath, and "In this moment I am safe," on the out-breath. Derek began to experience some relief within the first few weeks of practicing these skills, with improved sleep and fewer physical symptoms of anxiety.

Next, the therapist worked with Derek around acceptance practices. Via the metaphor of the Chinese finger trap and tug-of-war script, Derek began to find ways to release his thoughts from the repetitive negative cycle and shift his focus onto the present moment, using his five senses. These techniques helped him feel less reactive and hyper-aroused both at home and at work. After several months of focusing on mindfulness and acceptance practices, Derek experienced greater overall well-being. He began to re-engage with his family and friends and felt less irritable and reactive.

Tran

Tran is a 54-year-old working in the field of social work. Recently, Tran found that he was feeling more irritable than usual and began to dread the workday. He noted he felt overly frustrated with his clients and began calling in sick regularly. During these sick days, Tran would stay in bed and watch TV, even though there was nothing necessarily physically wrong. This was beginning to impact both his career and also his relationship with his partner.

Tran had heard about mindfulness and acceptance practices through a webinar that had been offered through his workplace. In that webinar, he learned the signs and symptoms of burnout, and he realized that he was experiencing many of those symptoms. Tran decided to take a weekend workshop on mindfulness training, and he found resources online on the pairing of mindfulness and acceptance techniques.

In the mindfulness training, Tran learned a variety of breathing exercises, such as 4x8 and A.N.B breathing, and various meditations, both focused and open awareness. He began practicing these each night before bed, noticing he slept better and felt more rested in the morning. In the morning, Tran began to use yoga stretches before breakfast, including downward dog, happy baby, cat-cow, and child's pose. His partner began to join his practice of yoga, which was helpful for their connection in their relationship. Together, they decided to attend a yoga retreat as their next vacation.

Through Tran's research about acceptance practices, he learned about the "clipboard technique" and began to utilize this at work. Tran began to actually bring a clipboard with him into his client meetings, which helped him not feel emotionally flooded or resistant to these meetings but instead to have acceptance around the challenges present in his work. He also began to watch his internal language for the word "but," and to replace that with the word "and." For instance, he internally rehearsed the phrase "I want to feel better AND I have a lot of stress at work," which left him options for how to better take care of himself through the use of mindfulness techniques. After a while, Tran began to regularly go to work and noted that his irritability and dread of the workday greatly diminished.

Concluding Comments

The stress response has developed over the period of human evolution as a mechanism that served to maintain life in physically threatening situations. It has arguably helped to ensure our success as a species. However, as society has evolved, stressors have changed. Over the course of time, situations wherein an immediate fight or flight response to preserve one's physical integrity have become less prevalent. In today's society, we more commonly experience social and mental stressors, to which the SNS-based stress response can be counterproductive, thereby generating the need to find ways to manage stress (Neece, 2013). This chapter has offered a number of mindfulness- and acceptance-based practices documented as effective in managing the stress response.

References

Ackerman, C. (2017, December 5). *9 self-compassion exercises & worksheets for increasing compassion.* PositivePsychology.com. https://positivepsychology.com/self-compassionexercises-worksheets/

Alexander, G. K., Rollins, K., Walker, D., Wong, L., & Pennings, J. (2015). Yoga for self-care and burnout prevention among nurses. *Workplace Health & Safety, 63*(10), 462–470. https://doi.org/10.1177/2165079915596102.

Asmundson, G. J., & Stein, M. B. (1994). Vagal attenuation in panic disorder: An assessment of parasympathetic nervous system function and subjective reactivity to respiratory manipulations. *Psychosomatic Medicine, 56*(3), 187–193. https://doi.org/10.1097/00006842-199405000-00002.

Biglan, A., Layton, G. L., Jones, L. B., Hankins, M., & Rusby, J. C. (2013). The value of workshops on psychological flexibility for early childhood special education staff. *Topics in Early Childhood Special Education, 32*(4), 196–210. https://doi.org/10.1177/0271121411425191.

Brinkborg, H., Michanek, J., Hesser, H., & Berglund, G. (2011). Acceptance and commitment therapy for the treatment of stress among social workers: A randomized controlled trial. *Behaviour Research and Therapy, 49*(6–7), 389–398. https://doi.org/10.1016/j.brat.2011.03.009.

Crane, R. S. (2017). Implementing mindfulness in the mainstream: Making the path by walkingit. *Mindfulness, 8*(3), 585–594. https://doi.org/10.1007/s12671-016-0632-7.

Duarte, J., & Pinto-Gouveia, J. (2017). The role of psychological factors in oncology nurses' burnout and compassion fatigue symptoms. *European Journal of Oncology Nursing, 28*, 114–121. https://doi.org/10.1016/j.ejon.2017.04.002.

Elliott, S. (2010, January 8). *Diaphragm mediates action of autonomic and enteric nervous systems.* BMED Report: Psychophysiology. https://www.bmedreport.com/archives/8309

Germer, C. (2009). *The mindful path to self-compassion: Freeing yourself from destructive thoughts and emotions.* Guilford Press.

Hanson, R., & Mendius. (2009). *Buddha's brain: The practical neuroscience of happiness, love and wisdom.* New Harbinger Publications.

Harris, R. (2009). *ACT made simple: A quick start guide to ACT basics and beyond.* New Harbinger.

Harris, A. R., Jennings, P. A., Katz, D. A., Abenavoli, R. M., & Greenberg, M. T. (2016). Promoting stress management and wellbeing in educators: Feasibility and efficacy of a school-based yoga and mindfulness intervention. *Mindfulness, 7*(1), 143–154. https://doi.org/10.1007/s12671-015-0451-2.

Hayes, S. C., Bissett, R., Roget, N., Padilla, M., Kohlenberg, B. S., Fisher, G., Masuda, A., Pistorello, J., Rye, A. K., Berry, K., & Niccolls, R. (2004). The impact of acceptance and commitment training and multicultural training on the stigmatizing attitudes and professional burn-out of substance abuse counselors. *Behavior Therapy, 35*(4), 821–835. https://doi.org/10.1016/S0005-7894(04)80022-4.

Hayes, S. C., Strosahl, K. D., & Wilson, K. G. (2012). *Acceptance and commitment therapy: An experiential approach to behavior change* (2nd ed.). Guilford Press.

Hinds, E., Jones, L. B., Gau, J. M., Forrester, K. K., & Biglan, A. (2015). Teacher distress and the role of experiential avoidance. *Psychology in the Schools, 52*(3), 284–297. https://doi.org/10.1002/pits.21821.

Holland, M. L., Malmberg, J., & Gimpel Peacock, G. (2017). *Emotional and behavioral problems of young children: Effective interventions in the preschool and kindergarten year* (2nd ed.). Guildford Press.

Lloyd, J., Bond, F. W., & Flaxman, P. E. (2013). The value of psychological flexibility: Examining psychological mechanisms underpinning a cognitive behavioural therapy intervention for burnout. *Work & Stress, 27*(2), 181–199. https://doi.org/10.1080/02678373.2013.782157.

McCurry, C. (2009). *Parenting your anxious child with mindfulness and acceptance: A powerful new approach to overcoming fear, panic, and worry using acceptance and commitment therapy*. New Harbinger.

Neece, C. L. (2013). Mindfulness-based stress reduction for parents of young children with developmental delays: Implications for parental mental health and child behavior problems. *Journal of Applied Research in Intellectual Disabilities, 27*(2), 174–186.

Nesse, R. M., Bhatnagar, S., & Ellis, B. (2016). Evolutionary origins and functions of the stress response system. In G. Fink (Ed.), *Stress: Concepts, cognition, emotion, and behavior* (pp. 95–101). Academic. https://doi.org/10.1016/B978-0-12-800951-2.00011-X.

Nosaka, M., & Okamura, H. (2015). A single session of an integrated yoga program as a stress management tool for school employees: Comparison of daily practice and nondaily practice of a yoga therapy program. *The Journal of Alternative and Complementary Medicine, 21*(7), 444–449. https://doi.org/10.1089/acm.2014.0289.

Oneda, B., Ortega, K. C., Gusmao, J. L., Araujo, T. G., & Mion, D. (2010). Sympathetic nerve activity is decreased during device-guided slow breathing. *Hypertension Research, 33*(7), 708–712. https://doi.org/10.1038/hr.2010.74.

Sinha, A., Deepak, D., & Gusain, V. (2013). Assessment of the effects of pranayama/alternate nostril breathing on the parasympathetic nervous system in young adults. *Journal of Clinical and Diagnostic Research, 7*(5), 821–823. https://doi.org/10.7860/JCDR/2013/4750.2948.

Smith, S. T. (2011). *The user's guide to the human mind: Why our brains make us unhappy, anxious, and neurotic and what we can do about it*. New Harbinger.

Telles, S., Sharma, S. K., & Balkrishna, A. (2014). Blood pressure and heart rate variability during yoga-based alternate nostril breathing practice and breath awareness. *Medical Science Monitor Basic Research, 20*, 184–193. https://doi.org/10.12659/MSMBR.892063.

Tolle, E. (1999). *The power of now: A guide to spiritual enlightenment*. New World Library.

Walker, J., & Pacik, D. (2017). Controlled rhythmic yogic breathing as complementary treatment for post-traumatic stress disorder in military veterans: A case series. *Medical Acupuncture, 29*(4), 232–238. https://doi.org/10.1089/acu.2017.1215.

Zelano, C., Jiang, H., Zhou, G., Arora, N., Schuele, S., Rosenow, J., & Gottfried, J. A. (2016). Nasal respiration entrains human limbic oscillations and modulates cognitive function. *Journal of Neuroscience, 36*(49), 12448–12467. https://doi.org/10.1523/JNEUROSCI.2586-16.2016.

Chapter 4
Defusion and Cognitive Techniques

This chapter highlights cognitive techniques, including defusion practices, as they relate to compassion fatigue and burnout. The role of thoughts in stress, trauma, and burnout is explored. Cognitive approaches, including defusion techniques, are defined and reviewed, with practical tools and case examples to highlight the use of these approaches in intervening in burnout and TRES.

The Role of Thoughts in Stress

It is common for people to focus their attention on the contents of their mind (thoughts, memories, assumptions, beliefs, images, etc.) rather than what is experienced through the five senses. Decisions and actions are, therefore, often based on one's internal experience (thoughts, memories, etc.) rather than what is actually going on around them. These internal experiences can become rigid and can often be a primary lens by which situations are experienced, also called cognitive fusion. Harris (2009) notes that in this state of cognitive fusion thoughts can seem like absolute truth or rules one must follow. Cognitive fusion is intricately related to words that people tell themselves. This higher order cognitive function can interfere with the ability to clearly see situations or circumstances and can lead to misleading subsequent feelings and behaviors. For instance, we might relate the word "worthless" to our lack of ability to perform a function at our job, and then by extension begin to relate that word "worthless" to our lives as a whole.

As discussed in Chap. 3, our bodies physically react to stressors by activating our sympathetic nervous system (SNS) or fight, flight, or freeze response. This prepares our bodies to run from or fight threats in our environment and was important to our ancestors who were often exposed to physical threats (Nesse et al., 2016). While SNS activation has proved evolutionarily helpful in our survival as a species, in today's society, it has become counterproductive and even harmful to our mental

M. L. Holland et al., *Burnout and Trauma Related Employment Stress*,
https://doi.org/10.1007/978-3-030-83492-0_4

and physical health when activated over long periods of time. When our SNS activation is prolonged, strong, and frequent, we experience toxic stress. Toxic stress is related to relational, physical, emotional, behavioral, psychological, and cognitive difficulties (National Child Traumatic Stress Network, n.d.). Toxic stress can be a consequence of real threats in our environment such as trauma exposure (e.g., experiencing abuse or neglect). However, threatening, unpleasant, or uncomfortable thoughts are enough to activate the body's stress response system leading to burnout and TRES.

Cognitive Approaches

Cognitive behavior therapy (CBT) has been found to be effective for a number of problems (e.g., anxiety, depression, and substance use disorders). CBT addresses psychological problems, which are related to unhelpful thought and behavior patterns. CBT involves changing thinking patterns, which can include recognizing and evaluating unhelpful thoughts, understanding behaviors and motivation, problem solving, and recognizing strengths. To challenge unhelpful thought patterns, CBT involves noticing automatic thoughts, evaluating whether thoughts are helpful or true, and then changing unhelpful thoughts to become more realistic and adaptive (American Psychological Association, 2021).

Cognitive Defusion in ACT

While CBT requires the editing and altering of unhelpful thoughts, ACT works to reduce the power and hold of unhelpful thoughts, so that they are easier to accept (Deacon et al., 2011). Cognitive defusion in ACT focuses on the fact that thoughts are just thoughts (images or words that occur in the mind) and have no meaning or power until we assign it. Cognitive defusion techniques are purposed to create space or distance between ourselves and our thoughts. Therefore, when unhelpful thoughts arise, they are more easily recognized as thoughts, not truths or facts that define us. A summary of cognitive defusion strategies covered in this chapter is found in Table 4.1.

Leaves on a Stream Meditation

Using visualization is a common meditation technique to assist with reducing attachment to thoughts, thereby increasing defusion. For example, when you have a thought during meditation, you are guided to notice the thought and, instead of creating stories in your head off of that thought, imagine physicalizing the thought and

Table 4.1 Summary of cognitive defusion strategies in this chapter

Strategies	Definitions	Target process/outcome
Leaves on a stream	A meditation using the imagery of placing a thought on a floating leaf on a stream, noticing the thought without further entertaining it, and bringing your attention back to the present moment	To notice thoughts without attachment to the thought, thereby bringing you back to the present moment
Thought bubble meditation and mental hands	Meditations that can assist you in noticing thought without attaching to the thought	To notice thoughts without attaching to the thought, thereby bringing you back to the present moment
Sunglasses metaphor	A metaphor noting that thinking minds are like the lenses of sunglasses: They can change the perspective of how things are seen around us	Recognizing how thoughts "color" our experience, especially negatively
I am labels	A technique to help recognize the power of words. Instead of saying "I'm going to fail," say, "I'm having the thought that I'm going to fail," thereby creating space between you and the thought	Changing "I AM" language to "I am having the thought that" or "having symptoms of"
Numbers games	A technique that demonstrates that there is no delete button for thoughts	Recognizing how we cannot make our thoughts disappear
Silly voice	A technique involving changing the tone of the internal message to help create more flexibility in thinking	To assist you in further defusion of thought
Milk technique	An activity involving the repetition of a word, which over time weakens the attachment between the word and its meaning	To assist you in further defusion of thought
Physicalizing the thought	A technique wherein imagery is used to physicalize the thought or feeling, such as giving it color, form, speed, etc.	To imagine the thought as an external entity
Parables	A parable that speaks to the fight that goes on inside of us with regard to what thoughts we attach to in our minds	To assist you in further defusion of thought
Traffic on the street	The idea that our thoughts are like cars in traffic, distracting us from the present moment and taking us on various trips and detours	To assist you in further defusion of thought
Thanking your mind	Your brain thinks it is helping by repeating these thoughts to you. Simply thank it, then refocus on the present moment and what you can get accomplished	To assist you in further defusion of thought
Type it out	Imagine your thought on a computer screen, then change it by altering the font size, formatting, and color	To assist you in further defusion of thought

do something with it in your visual imagination. Many mindfulness meditations use the imagery of placing that thought in a bubble, on a cloud, or on a floating leaf on a stream. Noticing the thought without further entertaining it brings the attention back to the present moment. A common ACT meditation is "Leaves on the Stream" (Harris, 2009), as offered in Table 4.2.

Thought Bubble Meditation and Mental Hands

The Thought Bubble Meditation can assist you in noticing thought without becoming attached to the thought and is similar to the Leaves on the Stream exercise. A sample script for the Thought Bubble Meditation is offered in Table 4.3.

A second form of imagery that can help explore attachment to thought in the mind involves the idea that the mind has "mental hands." When thoughts arise, we have a choice. We can grab onto the thought with our mental hands and create a story for ourselves around it, or we can open our hands to the thought and release it into the atmosphere. We have found actually physically opening your hands at the same time you are letting out an outbreath (e.g., when using 4x8 breathing) can be useful in physicalizing the thought and letting it go.

Table 4.2 Sample leaves on the stream meditation script

Begin to take deep, 4X8 breaths. Imagine you are sitting by a peaceful, slow moving stream. The water is flowing over stones and past tall trees. Every once in a while, a large leaf drops into the stream. It floats away on the surface of the water down the river. Imagine you are watching the leaves float by.
Now become aware of your thoughts. Each time a thought comes into your mind, imagine placing the thought on one of the leaves. Stay beside the stream and watch the leaves float by. Try not to make the stream go faster or slower, and do not try to change what thoughts you are placing onto the leaves.
If you notice you have mentally left your spot by the stream, just notice that this has happened. Gently bring yourself back to the stream and continue placing your thoughts onto the leaves.
Now slowly bring your awareness back into the room.

Table 4.3 Sample thought bubble meditation script

Begin by taking 4X8 breaths. As you breathe, thoughts may come into your mind. When a thought comes into your mind, imagine putting that thought in a bubble. Try not to think more about the thought. Instead, just notice it floating in the bubble. Now, watch the thought float away in the bubble. As the next thought comes into your head, imagine putting that thought into a bubble, and watch it float away.

Sunglasses Metaphor

The sunglasses metaphor is intended to help individuals understand that their thinking minds are like the lenses of sunglasses. They can change the perspective of how you see the world around you. For example, if you put on very dark sunglasses, the world around you would suddenly appear dark. Conversely, if you wore red, green, or blue sunglasses, the world around you would have hues of those colors. Often what we see is colored by the lens of our thinking minds. For example, if we think "this is going to be a terrible day," when we wake up, how might this lens taint our experience of the rest of the day? Thoughts are like the colors of the glasses; they can change, alter, and distort how things may actually be and look.

I Am Labels

The only thing that we do know that we actually "are" is human. Almost everything else is alterable. Often, we use language that labels our identity when describing an alterable feature of who we are. For example, when introducing yourself you may say, "I am a teacher" or "I am a physician." When in reality, being a teacher or a physician is what you do as a job (and it can be changed) not who you are as a person. You can apply flexibility in your thinking when confronted with an "I am" thought. For example, when you have the thought, "I am anxious," you can adjust your thinking in the following way: "I am having the thought that I am anxious. It is just a thought, like any other thought. Now I will focus on what can help me to feel calm." This shift in thinking can help add emotional distance between the label and the experience of it in the moment (Hayes, 2004). In this way, the thought becomes less defining and opens up other possibilities (e.g., instead of "I am stupid," you can resource ways of better solving problems and brainstorming actionable solutions).

Numbers Game

With this technique, we introduce the idea that there is no delete button to use for thoughts (Hayes, 2005). This becomes especially important when you have been actively working on mindfulness and ACT techniques but are bothered that you still have negative thoughts. A sample script for the numbers game is offered in Table 4.4. After playing the numbers game, it is recommended you move into other defusion techniques, such as Silly Voice or Physicalizing the Thought (both introduced next), to assist with creating flexibility in your thinking pattern.

Table 4.4 Sample numbers game script

It is challenging to keep remembering thoughts and things that have happened to you, even when you try not to. Imagine this: If I were to ask you to say back the following numbers, 1, 2, 3, you would likely say… "Yes, 1, 2, 3." If asked at the end of the day, would you still be able to recall those three numbers? I am guessing you could. And, if in a week, I called and told you, "Hey, I have an extra $10,000 dollars in my bank account, and I would love to give it to you if you could try and remember those numbers you repeated during our time together, do you think it is possible you might remember them?" You probably could. And likely these numbers do not really mean anything to you besides just being numbers in a row.

So, if you can remember something that is not all that meaningful, for a pretty long time, it would be likely you will also continue to remember the hurtful things that you have experienced or a negative thought you have rehearsed to yourself over years.

So, it is not the forgetting of the memory or thought that is going to be your key to feeling healthier, it is going to be how much attention and weight you give it; how "sticky" the thought is and how fused it is in your mind.

Table 4.5 Sample Silly Voice Script

Imagine you are having the thought "I am a disappointment." Now imagine saying that thought in Mickey Mouse's voice, singing it to the tune of the Happy Birthday song, or using a slow-motion voice instead. Any voice you choose will work. The purpose is to not change the thought, but rather, to change its tone. This helps us to recognize it as just a thought, as opposed to an authoritative fact message.

Silly Voice

Often the painful thoughts we repeat to ourselves were rehearsed in an authoritative tone. Similar to "I am" statements, these negative thoughts can significantly taint how we experience the present moment and can lead to unhealthy or inconsistent emotional reactions and behaviors. Changing the tone of the internal message can help create more flexibility in thinking (Harris, 2009), as offered in Table 4.5.

Milk Technique

First used in the early 1900s (Tichener, 1916) to decrease the power of certain words, in this exercise, you quickly repeat the word "milk" over and over again for a minute in rapid succession. This action, over time, weakens the attachment between the word and its meaning, and the literal meaning of the word dissipates until it becomes simply noise. This technique is then generalized to words that may be triggering to you, such as "worthless" or "failure," to loosen those associations. These words then begin to be experienced in a less literal, more flexible way (Greco et al., 2008).

Physicalizing the Thought

Another technique to help with cognitive defusion is to "externalize" the problem (Winslade & Monk, 2007). This involves using imagery to physicalize a thought or feeling, such as giving it color, texture, or speed. Hayes (2005) notes that "when we look at objects external to ourselves, we do not take them to be self-referential" (p. 137). For example, if you were walking down the street and noticed a pile of trash, you would not tell yourself that you "are trash." However, when you have a negative thought or feeling about yourself, you may experience fusion around that thought or feeling and believe that you are, indeed, trash or a terrible person. A sample script illustrating this technique is offered in Table 4.6. This exercise can help you with no longer "being" your emotions but, instead, recognizing your emotion as "being in the room." In doing so, you can reduce the experience of the emotions and assist yourself in bringing in coping tools for how to increase wellness.

Parables

Parables are commonly used in ACT therapy and can be used to assist in examining your attachment to thought. One such parable, found below, discusses turning inward as opposed to being frozen in fear or running away from challenges.

> *One day, Mr. Turtle and Mr. Fox met in the forest. Mr. Fox thought, "I'm going to have a good meal today." And Mr. Turtle thought "Oh, my goodness. My enemy is out there. Shall I freeze? I will be eaten. Shall I run? I'm not fast enough." So, instead he went inside his shell. Mr. Fox paced round and round Mr. Turtle, but eventually he got tired of waiting and went away.* -Adapted from Kiourtzidis (2020)

The fox in this parable represents your challenge at hand. The idea here is to be like Mr. Turtle and to mindfully stay present and observe, as opposed to feeling flooded with fear and freezing or running away from your problems.

Another parable commonly retold in various iterations is noted below:

> *Question 1. What is the sound of one hand clapping?*
> *Answer: The sound of one hand clapping is the sound of one hand clapping.*
>
> *Question 2: What is the sound of one person making a mistake?*
> *Answer: The sound of one person making a mistake is the sound of one person making a mistake.*
>
> *Question 3: What is the sound of me making a mistake?*
> *Answer: The sound of "I shouldn't have done that," the sound of "I am a bad person," the sound of "I don't know what to do," the sound of "I hate myself," the sound of "I should just give up," and the sound of my failure.*
>
> *-unknown*

Table 4.6 Sample script for physicalizing the thought

Imagine an uncomfortable feeling. Now, imagine placing that feeling in front of you. Notice the color of it, its size, and its shape. Does it have any motion or speed? What is its texture? The next time you have this feeling, imagine this image and tell yourself that this feeling is in the room, not "I am" this feeling.

This passage powerfully illustrates how cognitive fusion can negatively impact our perception and behaviors. Note the "I am" labels and negative thoughts that will likely interfere with subsequent decisions. In the ACT approach, the content of the thought is not what is problematic; instead, it is the relationship or "fusion" with the thought that is important.

Traffic on the Street Meditation

A relatively simple meditation metaphor, titled "Changing Perspective" is offered on the app Headspace (2021). This metaphor includes the idea that our thoughts are like cars in traffic, distracting us from the present moment and taking us on various trips and detours (often to our detriment). Table 4.7 is an adaptation of a transcript from a Headspace (2017) YouTube video.

Thanking Your Mind

As overviewed in prior sections, we tend to either feel distracted and flooded by negative thoughts or, alternatively, we try and push away thoughts that are unwanted. For example, the thought "I will never finish all of this work" is unhelpful and prescribes a negative outcome. Trying to distract ourselves from the thought, or rehearsing it as a mantra of sorts, will leave us in less than full health, all the while likely remaining feeling stuck in our situation. The next time an unhelpful thought pops into your head, try saying, "Thank you, mind." Your brain thinks it is helping by repeating these thoughts to you. Simply thank it, then refocus on the present moment and what it is that you want to bring your attention toward.

Table 4.7 Changing perspective transcript

Imagine sitting on the side of a busy road and all you have to do is sit and watch the cars pass by. The passing cars represent your thoughts and feelings. Sounds simple, right? But watching the movement of the traffic can feel unsettling. So, you run out into the road and try to stop the cars or maybe even chase after a few of the cars. Even though the idea was to just sit there and watch. And you're running around adds to your restless feelings. So, the goal is about changing your relationship with the passing thoughts and feelings like the cars driving by you. Simply learning to view them. Doing this brings you back to the present moment. You will sometimes become distracted during the exercise. But as soon as you remember, you can come back to the side of the road again and just watch the traffic go by you.

Type It Out

Another way to create separation between ourselves and our challenging or painful thoughts is to type it out. This exercise asks you to imagine or type your thought on a computer screen and then alter it by changing the font size, format, and color. By visually altering the typography of our thoughts, we can lessen our emotional and behavioral reactions to them. Figure 4.1 illustrates this technique.

I AM A FAILURE

I am a failure   I am a failure

I am a failure

I AM A FAILURE   **I am a failure**   I AM A FAILURE

Fig. 4.1 Sample type it out exercise result

Case Examples

Sophia

Sophia, a 26-year-old resident in a nursing program, began to seriously question her desire to continue in her academic program and career. Sophia began to experience physical and emotional exhaustion, a loss of meaning in her work, and difficulty remembering things. She was, at times, working long hours with patients often in critical condition. Sophia began to feel worthless in her role at the hospital due to the nature of her work with very ill patients. This began to take a toll on her, and she socially isolated herself. Sophia also noticed that she no longer enjoyed engaging in activities that used to bring her pleasure, such as running and getting together with friends for coffee. The attending physician began to notice Sophia's symptoms of isolating behavior at work, fatigue, and depressed mood. They suggested that she meet with a counselor through her employee assistance program (EAP) to get some support.

Upon meeting Sophia, the EAP counselor noted Sophia had symptoms of both burnout and TRES. Sophia noted that she often had the thought of "being worthless" and feeling flooded with negative thinking. The counselor decided to use ACT therapy, and, because they only had a limited number of sessions, he primarily focused on mindfulness, acceptance, and defusion techniques with Sophia, giving her outside reading materials to examine her values and goals. The counselor began with 4 X 8 breathing (see Chap. 3) and incorporated the Leaves on the Stream Meditation into their work. Through this exercise, Sophia was able to begin to get distance from her thought of "being worthless." To help Sophia loosen her fusion with her negative thinking overall, the counselor introduced her to the Traffic on the Street Meditation and, in between sessions, Sophia began to use the phone app, Headspace to continue this defusion work at home.

To further work with Sophia's thought that she is worthless, the counselor introduced several other acceptance and defusion techniques. The counselor worked with Sophia on the Clipboard Technique (see Chap. 3), helping her to recognize how she has been flooding herself with her negative feelings about her work. Through this exercise, Sophia was able to loosen her attachment around the things that were challenging to her about her job (e.g., the premorbid severity of the health of her patients), and she was able to see more clearly her role as a helper (as opposed to feeling useless or worthless). Once Sophia could experience some detachment from her thought of being worthless, the counselor modeled for Sophia the use of the Silly Voice technique to help further decrease her fusion around the thought of being "worthless." Together they practiced the voice of Mickey Mouse saying, "I am worthless," which made Sophia laugh. She noted she could see how, when she said it to herself, it was in a serious, commanding internal voice. Using the silly voice allowed Sophia to see the thought as less realistic and more as just a thought she was having. At this point, the counselor moved into physicalizing the thought of "worthless" and asked her what that thought would look like if it were in the room. Sophia, though uncomfortable at first with this new idea, began to build out a picture of what "worthless" would be if it were a physical object. She described that it would be gray in color, the texture of a cloud, and would be cold in temperature. Once Sophia could externalize the thought of "worthless" into the room, the counselor was able to help her practice the language of "When I notice the thought 'worthless'" as opposed to "I am worthless."

Sophia noted in her next session with the counselor that she was still having the thought that she was "worthless" at work. The counselor played "The Numbers Game" to demonstrate how there is no delete button on thoughts, and instead, we have to learn how to reduce our attachment to the thoughts we are having. At this point, Sophia was instructed to ask herself, "What am I needing to best support myself when I notice the thought 'worthless'"? This led to a discussion of self-care techniques Sophia could use, such as replacing the thought with healthier, more realistic thinking, (e.g., I have stress AND I am competent and worthy), texting a friend, or going for a walk or run.

At the conclusion of the EAP sessions, Sophia was given the book, "Get Out of Your Mind and Into Your Life: The New Acceptance and Commitment Therapy," by Hayes (2005). Sophia was also given the homework assignment to begin to exercise again and reconnect with friends, two areas Sophia had begun to neglect, which left her feeling out of balance in her life. Through Sophia's independent work using the book and various meditations, she noticed she was no longer feeling as fatigued and she was able to reconnect with things that used to bring her pleasure. As a result of working through the book, Sophia began to more fully focus on her values that brought her into nursing (see Chap. 5) and overall felt healthier with improved well-being.

Mohammed

Mohammed, a 55-year-old clinical psychologist, attended a continuing education (CE) course on burnout in the helping professions. Mohammed was surprised to discover he rated himself as experiencing significant symptoms of burnout on the Maslach Burnout Inventory (see Chap. 7). Specifically, he noted high levels of stress, muscle tension, mental, physical and emotional exhaustion, and negative thoughts as they related to his work. Lately, he had begun self-talk of, "I am stressed," and "I don't want to go into work today." In the CE course he learned about the use of ACT as an intervention for supporting helpers with burnout. For Mohammed, the tenets behind mindfulness and defusion techniques registered with him as possible promising interventions to try.

Mohammed started by attending yoga classes at his local community center and incorporating mindfulness outside of his classes, namely via regularly practicing 4X8 breathing. Almost immediately, Mohammed noted a decrease in his feelings of stress, physical fatigue, and tension. Using 4X8 breaths throughout the day (not just when he was feeling stress) was helpful to reduce his overall SNS activity. Through yoga, he realized how much tension he was holding onto in his neck and shoulders. He began to feel more relaxed and fewer physical symptoms of stress.

Next, Mohammed began implementing a variety of defusion techniques into his daily life. What particularly resonated with him was the idea behind "I Am" labels. He noticed he used a lot of "fused" self-talk, such as "I am stressed," which led him to further focusing on these symptoms of stress without identifying ways of helping himself. He began to replace these "I Am" thoughts with, "I am having the thought that I am stressed," enabling him to view these as just thoughts he was having as opposed to immutable traits. He used the "Thanking Your Mind" exercise when having the thought that he was experiencing stress, wherein he would tell himself, "Thank you, mind, for letting me know I need to engage in self-care at this time." This helped him to turn toward his list of self-care goals (see Chap. 5) to best support his well-being.

Over time, Mohammed began to experience a decrease in burnout symptoms and felt renewed energy toward his work. As a part of a daily wellness routine, including focusing on his nutrition and sleep, he incorporated 4X8 breathing with morning yoga and defusion techniques. He began to share the techniques he learned with other providers in his practice to help them with their stress levels as well.

Concluding Comments

As discussed in Chap. 3, the society that most of us live within has to a certain extent made the stress response counter-productive. Consequently, there is a need for strategies that can help to manage stress and, in particular, the stress associated with burnout and TRES. This chapter has addressed the role of unhelpful thinking or thoughts that is often associated with counter-productive stress and has emphasized cognitive approaches for doing so, particularly emphasizing defusion techniques. As is the case with mindfulness-based approaches, these strategies are conveniently with you wherever you go. While ideally made a regular part of a daily mental wellness routine, they can be deployed at the time and in the place wherein the signs and symptoms of burnout and TRES are observed.

References

American Psychological Association. (2021). *What is cognitive behavioral therapy?* https://www.apa.org/ptsd-guideline/patients-and-families/cognitive-behavioral

Deacon, B. J., Fawzy, T. I., Lickel, J. J., & Wolitzky-Taylor, K. B. (2011). Cognitive defusion versus cognitive restructuring in the treatment of negative self-referential thoughts: An investigation of process and outcome. *Journal of Cognitive Psychotherapy: An International Quarterly, 25*(3), 218–232. https://doi.org/10.1891/0889-8391.25.3.218.

Greco, L. A., Barnett, E. R., Blomquist, K. K., & Gevers, A. (2008). Acceptance, body image, and health in adolescence. In L. A. Greco & S. C. Hayes (Eds.), *Acceptance & mindfulness treatments for children and adolescents: A practitioner's guide* (pp. 187–214). New Harbinger.

Harris, R. (2009). *ACT made simple: A quick start guide to ACT basics and beyond.* New Harbinger.

Hayes, S. C. (2004). Acceptance and commitment therapy. In S. C. Hayes, V. M. Follette, & M. M. Linehan (Eds.), *Mindfulness and acceptance: Expanding the cognitive-behavioral tradition* (pp. 1–29). Guilford Press.

Hayes, S. C. (2005). *Get out of your mind and into your life: The new acceptance and commitment therapy.* New Harbinger.

Headspace, Inc. (2017, August 17). *Changing perspective* [video]. https://www.youtube.com/watch?v=iN6g2mr0p3Q

Headspace, Inc. (2021). https://www.headspace.com

Kiourtzidis, G. (2020). *On mindfulness.* http://allandeverything.org/on-mindfulness/

National Child Traumatic Stress Network. (n.d.). *Complex trauma.* https://www.nctsn.org/what-is-child-trauma/trauma-types/complex-trauma

Nesse, R. M., Bhatnagar, S., & Ellis, B. (2016). Evolutionary origins and functions of the stress response system. In G. Fink (Ed.), *Stress: Concepts, cognition, emotion, and behavior* (pp. 95–101). Academic. https://doi.org/10.1016/B978-0-12-800951-2.00011-X.

Tichener, E. B. (1916). *A text-book of psychology.* Macmillan.

Winslade, J. M., & Monk, G. D. (2007). *Narrative counseling in schools: Powerful & brief* (2nd ed.). Corwin Press.

Chapter 5
Commitment: Values and Professional Goal Setting

This chapter reviews the use of commitment practices as they relate to prevention and intervention in burnout and TRES, specifically how clarifying our values influences our personal and professional goals, thereby assisting us in our commitment to living a values-based life. To best identify our values, it is important to understand how we conceptualize ourselves (self-as-context) and how our self-concept can play a role in our professional health and well-being. Heartfulness, gratitude, and compassion satisfaction are explored in this idea of self-as-context as buffers against burnout and TRES, along with temporary and enduring self-care strategies. Identifying personal and professional values to set values-based goals is a focus, which can realign us in a healthy way with our helper identity.

Commitment

An important step in ACT is to foster commitment to our goals. Commitment in ACT means to engage in actions based on values that assist in setting and progressing from our short-term to long-term goals. This is critical as it relates to work related stress and fatigue, as we often lose sight of our values-based goals and, therefore, lose our commitment to important aspects of our lives, both personally and professionally. At times when we become stuck in our scripts about who we are in our jobs or lives, we continue to narrate a negative, depleting story to ourselves about our situation. Therefore, it is important to understand how we define ourselves (self-as-context), in that we are not the content of our thoughts and feelings, but rather the observer or experiencer of them. In this way, we can begin to uncover what we truly value, without being stuck in our narratives. Fostering compassion satisfaction, heartfulness, and gratitude can be important processes by which to alter the scripts about ourselves (Emmons & McCullough, 2003).

Self-as-Context

Self-as-Context refers to our "observing self" in ACT (Hayes et al., 2012). The idea of the "observing self" is important because, while we can notice the contents of our consciousness and experience, we are not those contents themselves. We have a thought, but we are more than that experience, just in the way that we have feet, but we are more than just our feet. Thoughts do not observe themselves, emotions do not feel themselves, and physical pain does not experience itself; we are the observer of these experiences. Throughout our lives, we can notice the presence of an "observing self," or our ability to view our own experience as we might view it as the experience of someone else. This allows us to step out of our own personal narratives (our thinking minds) about who we are, such as the "I am" labels (e.g., "I am lazy") that oftentimes can lead to feelings such as guilt, shame, and anxiety. The more that we can create defusion around the habitual stories we tell ourselves about ourselves, the more that we can observe those stories instead of "being" those experiences (Hayes & Greco, 2008). In this way, we begin to foster compassion and kindness toward ourselves.

Self-Kindness

In general, we tend to be able to put a supportive arm around a friend before ourselves. Western culture fosters an idea that we must remain stoic and silent toward our own suffering, focusing on "fixing" the problem as opposed to comforting ourselves. Unfortunately, these attitudes deny us of one of the most powerful coping mechanisms when dealing with challenge and difficulty, which is the ability to comfort ourselves when we are hurting and in need of care. We often focus on our struggles and challenges as if they are aberrations and assume that other people are having an easier time of it. This act of social comparison can lead us down the rabbit hole of not only punishing and berating ourselves for our problems but also isolating ourselves from others as we imagine their lives as being more ideal or perfect.

Self-kindness refers to the act of being supportive and sympathetic toward ourselves when noticing our personal shortcomings rather than focusing solely on fixing the problem or being harshly self-critical. Fostering self-compassion is expressed by engaging in internal dialogues (the stories we tell ourselves) that are encouraging and supportive rather than harsh or disparaging. Self-kindness and compassion involve acceptance that mistakes and failings are human and helps us approach them with understanding. When we foster warmth, gentleness, and sympathy from ourselves to ourselves, it is only then that true healing can occur (Neff & Tirch, 2013).

Heartfulness and Gratitude Activities

A primary tool for helping to foster kindness and compassion in our lives, for others, and ourselves is to engage in heartfulness and gratitude exercises. Gratitude involves awareness and appreciation of good things that happen, as well as taking time to express thanks (Park et al., 2004). Beyond fostering general well-being, gratitude has been found to be a buffer against burnout. Chan (2011) investigated an intervention focused on gratitude among teachers and its effect on burnout. Results found that participants in the intervention had increased positive affect and satisfaction with their jobs and life, especially among those who were lower on dispositional gratitude. In addition, workplace-specific gratitude predicted variables of burnout (e.g., emotional exhaustion and depersonalization) and job satisfaction when controlling for demographic (e.g., age), job contextual variables (e.g., supervisor support), and positive emotions (e.g., hope; Lanham et al., 2012).

Heartfulness means having a warm, heartfelt relationship with whatever is happening in our experience, internal or external. It means that we are developing the capacity to regard life with a sense of empathy and kindness (Sofer, 2016). Heartfulness activities have been found to be beneficial in producing positive mood, buffering stress and burnout, and increasing compassion for participants and those they care for (Emmons & McCullough, 2003; Klimecki et al., 2013). A 12-week study of heartfulness meditation with physicians and nurses in large community hospitals was conducted by Thimmapuram et al. (2017). Participants in the heartfulness group showed statistically significant improvement in emotional wellness and in their scores on the Maslach Burnout Inventory, whereas controls showed no significant changes in either wellness or burnout. In general, heartfulness has been found to be an important component in meditation and mindfulness as it seems to foster psychological well-being through a warm and aware attitude toward the self and others (Voci et al., 2019). Below are several heartfulness and gratitude activities to help foster self-compassion and kindness.

Gratitude Journaling

A relatively simple heartfulness activity that can be used is gratitude journaling. This journaling can be as simple as writing down one to three things you are grateful for every day before bed. Then, first thing the next morning, read the positive note to yourself to begin your day with a grateful outlook. You may focus your journaling on the workplace or other areas of life (Lanham et al., 2012).

Gratitude Anchors

Gratitude anchors involve selecting small moments in your day that cue awareness toward appreciation. Anchors may include the moment you sit down at your desk, buckle your seat belt, sit down to eat with family, or lay your head on your pillow (Branstetter, 2021). Allow the small anchors throughout your day to become a gratitude routine.

What Would I Tell a Good Friend?

This activity entails asking yourself in various situations, "What would I tell a dear friend, if they were experiencing what I am experiencing?" For example, if you are having the thought that you are failing in some way, instead of using your critical voice, ask yourself how you would support a friend if they were having that thought. Then, replace your critical thinking with the supportive language you would use toward your friend (Burns, 2017).

Letter to Self

Another exercise that can help to increase heartfulness and self-compassion is to write a letter to yourself from the perspective of a compassionate friend. In this three-step process, first think about the imperfections and insecurities that make you feel anxious or inadequate and take note of the emotions that come up around those thoughts. Next, write a supportive letter to yourself from the perspective of an unconditionally loving imaginary friend. This friend not only knows about your feelings of insecurity and inadequacies but also knows all about your gifts and strengths. The final step is to reread the letter after you have put it down and gotten some space from it (perhaps a day later). The key is to have intention in letting the words sink in from this uncondi-tionally loving friend in order to have the "friend's" compassion become your own self-compassion (Ackerman, 2017). You may also consider writing a gratitude letter to a specific person; this letter can be used as an exercise to cultivate personal gratitude or can be shared with the person it is written about.

Compassion Satisfaction

Compassion satisfaction is the positive experience of helping others (Thieleman & Cacciatore, 2014). As compassion satisfaction increases, compassion fatigue decreases. This relationship between compassion satisfaction and fatigue under-scores the importance of coping with unique work stressors while connecting to the positive and affirming aspects of the workplace. Research has shown self-compassion and purpose, mindful self-awareness, and supportive relationships to be the strongest mediators between compassion satisfaction and burnout. In addition, physical exercise, play, self-reflection, meditation, and rest not only reduce compassion fatigue but also increase compassion satisfaction (Hotchkiss, 2018).

Values

Values are our principles and ideals that give our lives direction and meaning. These principles and ideals tell us where to direct our energies in work, recreation, and relationships (e.g., goal formation; McCurry, 2009). Values reflect who or what is important and who or what we truly care about, not about what we want to get or achieve. Values are how you want to behave right now and for the rest of your life moving forward. For example, you may identify courage and kindness as values; these values become the framework for the way you choose to live your life, the goals you set out to accomplish, and how you go about accomplishing your goals. Common values include adventure, assertiveness, compassion, connection, creativity, curiosity, determination, enthusiasm, humor, persistence, respect, responsibility, safety, and trust (Harris, 2019). Table 5.1 lists the exercises designed to help identify personal core values that are discussed in this section.

Values List

One avenue for determining what you value is the creation of a values list (Harris, 2009). Some of the most commonly held values fall in the following areas: family relationships, friendships, romantic relationships, career, parenting, education,

Table 5.1 Values identification strategies

Strategies	Definitions	Target process/outcome
Values list	The creation of a values list	For all presenting concerns. Helps to identify core values
Eightieth birthday party	An activity wherein you imagine three people who, at your eightieth birthday, will stand up and give a speech about you, including what you stood for in your life. The descriptors that are included in the "speeches" are often the areas you most value	For all presenting concerns. Helps to identify core values
Remodeling the house	An activity wherein you imagine remodeling your home but realize your foundation is cracked. Attending first to your foundation (your values) is critical before further making decisions about the remodel	For all presenting concerns. Helps to recognize the importance of core values

recreation/leisure, spirituality, citizenship, and health/physical well-being (Hayes, 2005). Other areas can be added when appropriate. Identify the value areas that are most important to you by rank ordering them. You can list specific circumstances in each of the areas (such as, "my relationship with my spouse" "spending more time with my kids," or "my promotion at work") that are most salient at this time. Short-term to long-term goals can then be created based on the areas ranked as most important. You can also write the values areas on index cards and manually order them to create a visual hierarchy of those that are most important. Remember, some values may come into more focus at this time in your life than others, but it does not mean that you do not still hold all values as important. For example, when we have a sick loved one, we need to care for them; the value of "family relationships" may be at the top of our list and our current primary focus, though our career and other life values areas will still be included in the hierarchy.

Eightieth Birthday Party

The eightieth birthday party is a technique that can help in further exploring what you value (Harris, 2009). The idea here is to imagine three people who, at your eightieth birthday, stand up and give a speech about you, including what you stood for in your life. This is your fantasy, so you can include people who likely may not be alive at the time of this party (e.g., parents or grandparents) or who may not exist in this moment (e.g., a future life partner or child). The descriptors that are included in the "speeches" are often the areas that you most value. You can then formulate goals to support your values identified as most important.

Remodeling the House

Stoddard and Afari (2014) suggest imagining that you are planning to remodel your home. You are excited to design your kitchen, repaint the bedrooms, and choose new tile for the bathroom. You set your budget and hire your contractor, but as you begin the remodel, you discover there is a major crack in your home's foundation. You can rearrange the furniture and buy colorful curtains, but if the foundation of your home is broken, the structure ultimately starts to lean over or collapse. You will need to spend more money and time now to repair the foundation properly, which may mean you must hold off on purchasing the new appliances or refinishing hard-wood floors. However, at the end of the day, you will have a solid home if you first focus on the foundation.

Trying to make decisions on how to live your life without first determining what you value is like remodeling your home without first fixing the foundation. It is important to know what you stand for before you make decisions that may lead you in a direction not consistent with your foundation. Living a life consistent with your values does not mean that your choices and circumstances you face will be easy, but it means that even when things do not go according to plan, you still know what you stand for and maintain the foundation of your integrity.

Setting Values-Based Intentions and Goals

A key focus in ACT is setting goals guided by our values (Hayes et al., 2012). For example, you may have the wish to "be a good employee" or to "get a promotion at work." Your value of being industrious, hardworking, and dedicated would then direct your goals and actions (e.g., volunteering for extra assignments and being on time for work).

Setting Intentions

The idea behind setting intentions can be helpful in goal setting (Hayes et al., 2012). For the purposes of this book, an intention is a course of action that you intend to follow. These can vary from day to day and even hourly. The following includes possible intentions that can be areas you may want to focus on: health, calm, happiness, peace, and productivity.

There are various ways intentions can be used. For example, you can use the intention as a focused meditation, wherein you ask yourself what intention you would like to focus on that day and select techniques that can help to support that intention (e.g., if your intention is to be "calm," then you could focus on that word in your mindfulness and breathing activities; see Chap. 3). Intentions can also be used as a form of goal setting. For example, if we identify an intention of focusing on "health," then we can set short-term goals around that intention, such as eating more fruits and vegetables and planning to get to bed an hour earlier that night. We are most motivated to follow through on goals that lie in our values areas. The following section contains ideas for values-based goal setting.

Committed Action

Committed action is when we purposefully choose to engage in particular actions based on our values, even those that are difficult, in order to deliberately create a pattern of behavior that serves the value (Hayes et al., 2012). For instance, if you would like to focus on having more balance and well-being in your life, then you would make deliberate choices to integrate self-care each day into your schedule (e.g., setting a plan for regular walks, meditating in the morning). Remembering our values can assist us in making decisions we may find challenging or aversive. For example, you may find it easier to commit to getting up earlier in the morning, which can be aversive, by reminding yourself of your work values (e.g., responsibility).

Focusing on the values that brought you to your profession and setting attainable short-term goals based on these values (a key component in ACT) can be useful to reduce professional burnout. Values are always available to us, and we are able to choose to act on them in any given moment; goals help move our values to action by identifying things we are aiming to achieve or want in our future (Harris, 2019). Therefore, as discussed in the prior section of this chapter, it is important to clarify what values you would like to focus on to set your goals. Once you have done so, you move into committed action based on these values via the use of SMART goals.

SMART Goals

Goals are outcomes that require committed effort (Hayes et al., 2012). When goals are trivial, ambiguous, or unrealistic, they become almost impossible to obtain. Learning how to create and frame goals sets action planning into motion. Measuring progress enables goal tracking and informs needed adjustments to obtain more success. SMART goals provide a guide to develop goals that are specific, meaningful, adaptive, realistic, and occur within a time frame (Harris, 2009). SMART goal steps are offered in Table 5.2. Table 5.3 offers other helpful tips for goal setting.

Temporary Versus Enduring Self-Care Goals

Self-care strategies are exactly as they sound: ways of taking care of ourselves. Self-care activities may result in a range of different experiences, from going to the doctor to eating healthy, or engaging in pleasurable activities, such as meeting friends for dinner. There are two kinds of self-care strategies that will be overviewed in this section: temporary and enduring (Peeples, 2020).

Temporary self-care is activities or experiences that we look forward to or anticipate. During temporary self-care activities, dopamine and serotonin are released in our brains, then these neurotransmitters subside when we are finished. Examples of temporary self-care include going out to dinner with a friend; going for a swim, run, walk, or practicing yoga; and taking a weekend trip. Enduring self-care, on the other hand, are those things that we incorporate regularly, almost like habits. Engaging in enduring self-care, such as mindfulness, has been shown to permanently strengthen neurological functioning (Hölzel et al., 2011). Below is a list of examples for both temporary self-care and enduring self-care. Examples of enduring self-care (like habits) include setting out breakfast dishes and making your lunch the night before work, listening to music at your workplace, building time to make your favorite tea or coffee drink in the morning for commute, taking small breaks every

Table 5.2 Steps in establishing SMART goals

Step 1:	
S:	**Specific**: List the actions you will take, what or who is involved, and when and where the action will occur. An example of a nonspecific goal would be: "I will spend more time organizing my workspace." A specific goal is: "I will clean out all of the drawers of my desk on Monday afternoon and organize them according to the materials I need moving forward." Another example of a nonspecific goal could be: "I will exercise more." A specific goal: "I will walk at lunch today around the neighborhood by my office for 45 minutes."
M:	**Meaningful**: The goal should be aligned with your values. It is important that the goal is not a rigid rule, merely trying to please others, or trying to avoid discomfort or pain, as these are not meaningful premises. If you sense it lacks a sense of meaning or purpose, check in with yourself, and see if it is actually guided by your values.
A:	**Adaptive**: Determine if your goal, as far as you can predict, is likely to improve the quality of your life. If obstacles occur, can you continue to pursue your goal and be flexible in that pursuit? It is important that goals be adaptive to your situation.
R:	**Realistic**: The goal you set should be realistically achievable. Determine if you have the resources you may need to achieve your goal, such as skills, time, money, physical endurance, and support. If these resources are necessary but unavailable, you will need to change your goal to a more realistic one. The new goal might actually be to find the missing resources, such as exercising more, saving more money, or consulting with others.
T:	**Time-frame**: To increase the specificity of your goal, set a date and time for when you will execute your goal. If this is not possible, set as accurate a time frame as you can.

Step 2:
Write down a graduated series of goals, starting from tiny simple goals that can be achieved right away. Then work toward longer- and longer-term goals that may not be achieved for months or even years.
A goal I can accomplish in the next 24 hours is...
A goal I can accomplish in the next few days or several weeks is....
A goal I can accomplish in the next few weeks and months is....
A goal that I can accomplish in the next several months and year is...

Step 3:
Identify obstacles or barriers to your goals. It is important to be aware of barriers to implementing value-based your goal, such as extra work engagements popping up. At these times, it is important to make a commitment to refrain from engaging in experiential avoidance (e.g., giving up your goal completely by taking an all or nothing approach, such as, "if I can't walk for my full hour, then I won't walk at all") and to utilize mindfulness, acceptance, and cognitive defusion techniques to help with flexibility in your thinking. These obstacles or barriers are both internal (fears, avoiding change, negative self-talk, low self-efficacy, replaying unhelpful narratives, self-limiting beliefs, perfectionism, etc.) and external (finances, health issues, environmental changes, lack of support system, etc.). Consider how you might navigate these potential barriers recognizing that internal obstacles are within your control, while some external barriers may fall outside of your control. For example, you may be able to work through negative self-talk and continue to progress toward your goals, but do not have control over other people's actions, perceptions, and feelings.

Table 5.3 Other helpful goal setting tips

Find your audience: Telling other people about your goal and sharing your ongoing progress can increase commitment.
Rewards: Reward yourself for making progress toward your goal. Build in small rewards to help push you on. Examples include treating yourself to a special coffee drink or simply cheering yourself on (e.g., "Nicely done! You made a start!").
Document: Recording your progress by keeping a journal or graph that plots your progress can be reinforcing to your continuing your actions.

60–90 minutes for playful or restful activity, taking 4 X 8 breaths and using your five senses to regularly attend to the moment, lighting candles in your space, building in a lunch hour every day, and asking yourself, "What can I do in this moment to best support myself?" Ironically, studies have shown that individuals tend to abandon self-care during times they feel stressed or overwhelmed (Godfrey et al., 2010). Therefore, it is important to continue self-care strategies even (and most importantly) during times of stress or when we notice signs of burnout.

When Setbacks Happen

It can be challenging to continue to make progress and use our tools in the face of setbacks. Perhaps you forget to use your mindfulness skills when feeling physically anxious, or you once again begin to feel overwhelmed by your thoughts or a specific negative experience and neglect to use cognitive defusion techniques. Setbacks are inevitable, and we will encounter challenges on our paths toward our goals. It is at these times that we can be reminded of our work and practice the tools we learned in mindfulness and ACT (Hayes et al., 2012). Four metaphors, as summarized in the below Table 5.4, can assist us in recovering from setbacks: the Swamp Metaphor, Passengers on the Bus, The Flip Side of the Paper Technique, and Mountain Climbing Imagery.

The Swamp Metaphor Imagine you are beginning a journey to a beautiful mountain, with your goal being to reach the summit at the top. As you begin your hike, you come across a swamp that encircles the entire mountain. There is no way around it, and it completely blocks your path. At this point, you have a decision to make. Your first option is to give up, turn around, and go home, leaving behind the goal you were pursuing. Your second option is wading into the swamp, swimming around in it, and choosing to stay stuck. The third option is based on the ACT principles of acceptance; even though it is not what you had intended or wanted, you can acknowledge and have acceptance of the swamp and make the choice to move through it, continuing on your path once you reach the other side (Hayes et al., 2012).

Passengers on the Bus This can be a helpful metaphor in practicing letting go of our struggle with negative thoughts and feelings, giving us the energy and focus to

Table 5.4 ACT relapse prevention strategies

Strategies	Definitions	Target process/outcome
The swamp metaphor	Compare progress toward your goal to a hike toward the peak of a mountain; when setbacks happen, we have choices such as turning back and giving up, staying stuck in the swamp, or moving through it	A tangible image of grit and resilience toward goals
Passengers on the bus	The "passengers on the bus" metaphor involves the imagery of being a bus driver, and the passengers as your thoughts, with the driver continuing to move towards the destination – that is, their goal or value – even when the passengers are unruly or negative	Imaging or acting out disruptive thinking and practicing acceptance as you move toward your identified goals
Flip side of the paper	This technique uses one side of a piece of paper to write about a challenge you are having, and the other side of the paper to write the values area that challenge is related to, thereby determining if the value is important enough to shift your attachment to the challenge and persevere	To identify if the challenge is over-riding your core value. To either make a determined change in your life, or to change your attachment around the challenge
Mountain climbing metaphor	A useful metaphor for setbacks using the simple imagery of climbing a mountain	To more reasonably assess setbacks or challenges and see that it does not have to be couched as a failure, but instead as a detour on your path, one that may lead to even more progress in the end

be more engaged as we move toward our goals (Hayes et al., 2012). In this activity, think of yourself as the bus driver, and the passengers as your troubling or challenging thoughts, feelings, and memories. We want to drive our bus (our life) toward a goal-oriented direction, but there are times when passengers on our bus become angry and begin to challenge us as bus drivers by saying hurtful comments or demanding that the bus be taken in a certain direction. We may find ourselves arguing with the passengers and feeling overwhelmed, distracted, or flooded by their presence. Alternatively, we may strike a deal that we will drive the bus wherever the passengers want, so long as they sit back and stay quiet. We may also try and push the passengers off the bus. Using the ACT principles as we did in the Swamp Metaphor, we can also choose to acknowledge and have acceptance of the passengers on our bus as opposed to being reactive and engaged. Therefore, we can continue to drive our bus in the direction we would like to go (toward our goal).

Flip Side of the Paper A common ACT acceptance activity is the Flip Side of the Paper, also known as Two Sides of the Coin (LeJeune, 2020). This activity can be helpful in determining if the challenge or struggle you may be facing is in alignment (or not) of your valued life area. In this exercise you will start with a blank piece of paper and a pen. On one side of the paper, write down something you are struggling with. For example, the amount of paperwork that is required in your position or the number of patients you have to see in a day. Next, you will flip your paper over. On the other side of the paper, write down your life area that you value which relates to this challenge. For instance, in the above example, you would likely write, "my career" as your life area. Now, if you had the power to do so, would you crumple up and throw away the paper? You would be getting rid of the problem, but along with it, you would also be giving up the other side too, as they are linked.

If you said yes, you would crumple up and throw away the paper, this informs you that what you are doing may no longer be in alignment with your values and a change is necessary. However, if you want to continue at your job, the goal instead will be to do some more work around how much attachment there is for you around the problem area. By utilizing ACT exercises, you can create space to focus on what is within your control, enable problem solving to improve your situation, and move to a place of acceptance so that you can continue to take action, guided by your values.

Mountain Climbing Metaphor The mountain climbing metaphor entails imagining yourself hiking up a mountain toward your goal (Hayes et al., 2012). As you are climbing, you may run into detours, steep slopes wherein you need to adjust your footing, or even areas where the trail may drop back down the mountain before it continues up. Some trails include switchbacks, wherein the route winds back and forth and you get the sense that you are not going anywhere quickly. Likely at each point on your trail, you may have a different report of how things are going. At times you may feel discouraged, as if you are not making much progress at all. At others, you may experience setbacks, wherein you have to take a few steps down in order to regain your footing. At these points, it is important to recognize that all of these challenges are just part of the path. Sometimes, even, when we take a step back to regain our footing, we may find we are able to launch ourselves even higher up the mountain than we originally could have. If we can begin to accept that oftentimes our paths are not linear and also learn how to enjoy ourselves along the way to our goal (e.g., the scenery we pass and the people we may meet), then we can make the path itself our goal, not simply a means to an end.

Case Examples

Colette

Colette is a 42-year-old veterinarian who struggles with symptoms of burnout. Specifically, she has been flooded with anxiety-related symptoms, including muscle tension and headaches, along with racing thoughts, mental and physical exhaustion, and feeling a lack of purpose in her work. She realizes that she needs some help to be most successful at work and to improve her well-being. She chooses to use ACT interventions, including mindfulness, acceptance, and identifying values, due to her physical symptoms of anxiety, her racing thoughts, and her loss of purpose in her career.

Colette begins by paying attention to her breath. Regularly, she uses 4 X 8 diaphragmatic breathing throughout the day. This helps her to decrease her physical symptoms of anxiety. She then begins to pair these breaths several times a day with the internal meditation of, "In this moment I am calm," on the in-breath, and "In this moment I am relaxed," on the out-breath, thereby disrupting some of her repetitive negative thoughts. Colette, at the encouragement of her colleague Annalyn, also starts to attend yoga classes on Tuesday and Thursday evenings after work. Colette begins to notice a reduction in her muscle tension and begins to sleep better, which lessens her headaches and exhaustion. She also begins a practice of gratitude journaling at night.

Through the use of reading materials on acceptance work, Colette loosens her attachments to trying to "fix" all of the issues she was experiencing at work, and instead she moves toward acceptance of her current workload, acknowledging that not everything can be completed every day before she leaves for home. Using the imagery of "dropping the rope" with her repetitive, negative thoughts, Colette experiences a reduction in her anxious thinking.

Colette next works on focusing on her values that brought her into the veterinary profession, using the "Eightieth Birthday Party" activity to help her define what she values. Through this activity, she identified her values of helping others and being a strong advocate for animals. Feeling refocused on her core values in her profession allowed her to decrease her attachment to the more challenging aspects of her work and to focus on self-care. Through the use of SMART goals, Colette committed to a plan of both temporary and enduring self-care. Colette also uses the imagery of the "Passengers on the Bus" to assist her in remaining "in the driver's seat" as she moves toward these goals, reducing her attachment to her remaining negative thoughts.

After several months of using ACT as self-help strategies, Colette felt more energy and experienced fewer symptoms of burnout. She experienced a renewed sense of purpose in her work as a veterinarian.

Lamont

Lamont, a 38-year-old school psychologist, has a very high caseload of youth in foster care, many of whom have significant abuse histories. His individual therapy and assessment duties with these youth require that he collect detailed information about their traumatic experiences. As a consequence of this vicarious exposure to their abuse histories, Lamont noticed that he was having symptoms consistent with TRES. He was not sleeping well, he found himself dreading the workday, and he felt irritated toward the families with whom he worked, often avoiding meeting with them if possible. Lamont also noticed he felt overwhelmed with the amount of paperwork necessary to manage these cases. Lamont was familiar with TRES as he had taken a full-day seminar on stress in the helping professions at the national conference he attended last winter. Lamont decided to relook at the materials he received from the seminar to get some ideas for how to best help himself in this situation.

The seminar materials focused on ACT as an intervention for those in the helping professions who are experiencing TRES. Lamont decided to try some of the overviewed activities. He began a mindfulness practice using 4 X 8 breath, focusing on his five senses at various times throughout the day. For example, in between each student he worked with, he would take a few minutes to use his 4 X 8 breaths and would pay attention to what he was seeing, hearing, smelling, tasting, and touching in that moment. Lamont found that he soon felt less physically stressed and exhausted.

Lamont decided to use the "Flip Side of the Paper" technique to help him determine how he felt about his job in light of his TRES symptoms. On the one side of the paper, Lamont wrote, "my current caseload" as the challenge he is struggling with. On the other side, Lamont wrote, "my career" as the life area to which that challenge is related. Lamont asked himself if he would crumple up the paper, and immediately determined he would not. This helped Lamont turn toward what he did value about his career, which was the ability to help children. Lamont decided to use other strategies to help himself with thoughts about feeling overwhelmed at work. When Lamont noticed thoughts such as, "I can't do this job anymore," he asked himself what he would tell a good friend if they were in a similar situation. For instance, instead of telling his friend they should quit their job, he would offer supportive and helpful advice, such as focusing on self-care at this time, consider seeing a professional therapist, and perhaps taking a vacation. He also found the imagery of the "Swamp Metaphor" to be useful when he felt stuck in a part of his job, such as the amount of paperwork he had to do or his current high caseload. Lamont also decided to meet with his supervisor in order to achieve a more balanced caseload wherein he was not seeing the majority of youth who had high trauma histories.

Lamont began to feel less anxious and stressed and greater feelings of well-being at work. He was sleeping better and no longer dreaded the workday. Lamont continued to practice the breathing techniques regularly, even incorporating them into his therapy with the students with whom he worked.

Concluding Comments

With this chapter's discussion of commitment practices, we hope to have further supported the professional's ability to address the consequences of burnout and TRES. By helping to clarify values and professional goals, the individual is better able to appreciate what is important to them and why they work in a helping role and/or engage with clients who have experienced or are experiencing traumatic stress. To achieve this end, we recommend that professionals consider the heartfulness and gratitude activities and values identification strategies offered in this chapter. We do recognize that when it comes to these commitment practices, one size does not fit all and that each and every one of the strategies offered in this chapter will not work for everyone. Thus, we recommend that readers consider them as options offered for their consideration and that they select the approach that works best.

References

Ackerman, C. (2017, December 5). *9 self-compassion exercises & worksheets for increasing compassion.* PositivePsychology.com. https://positivepsychology.com/self-compassionexercises-worksheets/

Branstetter, R. (2021, March 16). *The science of happiness for school psychologists.* https://school-psych.com/course/the-science-of-happiness/

Burns, D. (2017, March/April). *When helping doesn't help: Why some clients may not want to change.* Psychotherapy Networker. https://www.psychotherapynetworker.org/magazine/article/1076/when-helping-doesnt-help

Chan, D. W. (2011). Burnout and life satisfaction: Does gratitude intervention make a difference among Chinese school teachers in Hong Kong? *Educational Psychology, 31*(7), 1–15. https://doi.org/10.1080/01443410.2011.608525.

Emmons, R. A., & McCullough, M. E. (2003). Counting blessings versus burdens: An experimental investigation of gratitude and subjective well-being in daily life. *Journal of Personality and Social Psychology, 84*(2), 377–389. https://doi.org/10.1037//0022-3514.84.2.377.

Godfrey, C. M., Harrison, M. B., Lysaght, R., Lamb, M., Graham, I. D., & Oakley, P. (2010). The experience of self-care: A systematic review. *JBI Library of Systematic Reviews, 8*(34), 1351–1460. https://doi.org/10.11124/01938924-201008340-00001.

Harris, R. (2009). *ACT made simple: A quick start guide to ACT basics and beyond.* New Harbinger.

Harris, A. R. (2019). *ACT made simple: An easy-to-read primer on acceptance and commitment therapy* (2nd ed.). New Harbinger.

Hayes, S. C. (2005). *Get out of your mind and into your life: The new acceptance and commitment therapy.* New Harbinger.

Hayes, S. C., & Greco, L. A. (2008). Acceptance and mindfulness for youth: It's time. In L. A. Greco & S. C. Hayes (Eds.), *Acceptance & mindfulness treatments for children and adolescents: A practitioner's guide* (pp. 3–13). New Harbinger.

Hayes, S. C., Strosahl, K. D., & Wilson, K. G. (2012). *Acceptance and commitment therapy: An experiential approach to behavior change* (2nd ed.). Guilford Press.

Hölzel, B. K., Carmody, J., Vangel, M., Congleton, C., Yerramsetti, S. M., Gard, T., & Lazar, S. W. (2011). Mindfulness practice leads to increases in regional brain gray matter density. *Psychiatry Research, 191*(1), 36–43. https://doi.org/10.1016/j.pscychresns.2010.08.006.

Hotchkiss, J. T. (2018). Mindful self-care and secondary traumatic stress mediate a relationship between compassion satisfaction and burnout risk among hospice care professionals. *American Journal of Hospice & Palliative Medicine, 35*(8), 1099–1108. https://doi.org/10.1177/1049909118756657.

Klimecki, O. M., Leiberg, S., Lamm, C., & Singer, T. (2013). Functional neural plasticity and associated changes changes in positive affect after compassion training. *Cerebral Cortex, 23*(7), 1552–1561. https://doi.org/10.1093/cercor/bhs142.

Lanham, M. E., Rye, M. S., Rimsky, L. S., & Weill, S. R. (2012). How gratitude relates to burnout and job satisfaction in mental health professionals. *Journal of Mental Health Counseling, 34*(4), 341–354. https://doi.org/10.17744/mehc.34.4.w35q80w11kgpqn26.

LeJeune, J. (2020). *Pain and values: Two sides of the same coin*. Portland Psychotherapy. https://portlandpsychotherapy.com/2012/06/pain-and-values-two-sides-same-coin-0/

McCurry, C. (2009). *Parenting your anxious child with mindfulness and acceptance: A powerful new approach to overcoming fear, panic, and worry using acceptance and commitment therapy*. New Harbinger.

Neff, K., & Tirch, D. (2013). Self-compassion and ACT. In T. B. Kashdan & J. Ciarrochi (Eds.), *The context press mindfulness and acceptance practica series. Mindfulness, acceptance, and positive psychology: The seven foundations of well-being* (pp. 78–106). New Harbinger.

Park, N., Peterson, G., & Seligman, M. E. P. (2004). Strengths of character and Well-being. *Journal of Social and Clinical Psychology, 23*(5), 603–619. https://doi.org/10.1521/jscp.23.5.603.50748.

Peeples, J. (2020). *Teaching through trauma: Educator self-care tip sheet*. California Teachers Association. https://www.cta.org/educator/posts/trauma-selfcare-tipsheet

Sofer, O.J. (2016, April 8). Heartfulness practice. *Mindful schools*. https://www.mindfulschools.org/personal-practice/heartfulness-practice/

Stoddard, J. A., & Afari, N. (2014). *The big book of ACT metaphors: A practitioner's guide to experiential exercises & metaphors in acceptance & commitment therapy*. New Harbinger.

Thieleman, K., & Cacciatore, J. (2014). Witness to suffering: Mindfulness and compassion fatigue among traumatic bereavement volunteers and professionals. *Journal of Social Work, 59*, 34–41. https://doi.org/10.1093/sw/swt044.

Thimmapuram, J., Pargament, R., Sibliss, K., Grim, R., Risques, R., & Toorens, E. (2017). Effect of heartfulness meditation on burnout, emotional wellness, and telomere length in health care professionals. *Journal of Community Hospital Internal Medicine Perspectives, 7*(1), 21–27. https://doi.org/10.1080/20009666.2016.1270806.

Voci, A., Veneziani, C. A., & Fuochi, G. (2019). Relating mindfulness, heartfulness, and psychological well-being: The role of self-compassion and gratitude. *Mindfulness, 10*, 339–351. https://doi.org/10.1007/s12671-018-0978-0.

Chapter 6
Organizational Strategies for Addressing Burnout and Trauma-Related Employment Stress

As was illustrated in Chap. 1, common to all forms of burnout and trauma-related employment stress is the fact that they are associated, with and can be exacerbated by, both individual and organizational factors. Thus, not only must there be a focus on the individual factors that lead to burnout and trauma-related employment stress, but also there must be a focus on the work environment (Maslach et al., 2001). In fact, it has been suggested that situational and organizational factors may play a greater role in burnout than do individual variables (Lasalvia et al., 2009). In other words, addressing these work-related injuries is not simply the individual professional's responsibility. To be effective, organizations themselves must strive to create a work environment that attends to these issues. Failure to do so negatively affects the individual, the organization, and its clients. In fact, just as self-care might be considered an ethical responsibility for the professional, attending to the systemic factors associated with burnout and TRES stress might be considered an ethical responsibility for the organization (Jirek, 2020; National Association of School Psychologists, 2020).

In this chapter, we provide an examination of how workplace environments and employers can address professional burnout and trauma-related employment stress. We examine the organizational variables (i.e., work and caseload, organizational bureaucracy, and availability of external supports) associated with these work-related injuries. From this discussion, we conclude the chapter with recommendations for the workplace environment that we judge will help to address the challenges of burnout and TRES.

M. L. Holland et al., *Burnout and Trauma Related Employment Stress*,
https://doi.org/10.1007/978-3-030-83492-0_6

Workload and Caseload

Both the total number of hours worked (workload; Maslach & Leiter, 2016; Okoli et al., 2019; Rupert et al., 2015) and the number of cases or clients that are a part of a workload (caseload; Kim & Lambie, 2018) have been implicated in professional burnout and TRES. These factors have been suggested to be directly related to the exhaustion element of burnout (Maslach et al., 2001). In the words of Vlăduţ and Kállay (2010, p. 265): "Too many simultaneous tasks, too tight deadlines, unfavorable work-environment, … impair the relationship between the employee and the job, leading to increased emotional exhaustion." For example, Acker (2010), who examined burnout among 591 social workers, found significant positive correlations between caseload size and burnout (in particular emotional exhaustion and depersonalization). Similarly, Newell and MacNeil (2010) found that the professional's perception of having an excessively high caseload was associated with burnout. Warren et al. (2013) reported that professionals working more than 35 h per week reported more burnout than did those working less than 35 h. Hu et al. (2016) found that working long hours (more than 40 h per week) correlated with professional burnout.

Beyond the number of hours worked and the number of cases assigned, it would appear that the type of work plays a role in burnout and TRES. For example, among counselors, it has been reported that excessive external demands and assignments, not directly associated with counseling clients (e.g., the school counselor who is assigned administrative tasks that limits direct student contact), increases risk for burnout (Holman et al., 2019; Kim & Lambie, 2018; Okoli et al., 2019). In addition, the type of clients found within the professional's caseload should be taken into account. Specifically, professionals who work with negative or stressful clients (Rupert et al., 2015) or whose caseloads have a high ratio of traumatized (vs. non-traumatized) clients (Hensel et al., 2015) are more likely to have symptoms of professional burnout and TRES.

Organizational Bureaucracy

In general, bureaucratic constraints (Newell & MacNeil, 2010) and greater amounts of administrative duties and paperwork are associated with exhaustion and reduced feelings of personal accomplishment (Rupert et al., 2015). The effects of excessive bureaucracy on burnout appear to be particularly problematic when the professional works in a setting wherein there is a lack of perceived control or influence over organizational procedures and policy (Newell & MacNeil, 2010; Yang & Hayes, 2020). When professionals judge that they have little ability to influence decisions that affect their work, the result is lower levels of job engagement (Maslach & Leiter, 2016; Maslach et al., 2001) and higher burnout. Conversely, professionals who report having more control over work tasks and how to fulfill their assigned duties, report less burnout (Aronsson et al., 2017; Lee & Ashforth, 1996; Rupert et al., 2015).

Related to the concept of having some say in (or control over) decisions that affect work is fairness, which is the extent to which the professional views decisions made within the work environment as being fair and equitable. Unfairness in organizational structure, procedures, and discipline are associated with burnout (Newell & MacNeil, 2010). For example, Maslach and Leiter (2016) offer:

> People use the quality of the procedures, and their own treatment during the decision-making process, as an index of their place in the community. Cynicism, anger and hostility are likely to arise when people feel they are not being treated with the appropriate respect. (p. 105)

To the extent the professional feels some degree of control over, or that they are empowered to make decisions that affect their work environment, the more they are likely to feel effective and to have an enhanced self-appraisal (Lee & Ashforth, 1996).

Support

Support, in particular well established and long-term social support, has long been suggested as a buffer against trauma-related stress (Brock et al., 2016; Lerias & Byrne, 2003; Lloyd et al., 2002; Ozer et al., 2003). Thus, it is not surprising to find that a lack of support is an important organizational factor in the development of burnout and TRES (Hensel et al., 2015). For example, Maslach et al. (2001, p. 415) offers that the loss of "...a sense of positive connection with others in the workplace," is associated with professional burnout. In contrast, Maslach and colleagues report individuals:

> ... function best when they share praise, comfort, happiness, and humor with people they like and respect. In addition to emotional exchange and instrumental assistance, this kind of social support reaffirms a person's membership in a group with a shared sense of values. (p. 415)

Professionals who perceive their employment environment to provide support have a greater sense of personal accomplishment and less exhaustion (Aronsson et al., 2017; Rupert et al., 2015). Conversely, those who perceive low levels of such support tend to report higher levels of exhaustion (Holman et al., 2019).

Supervisors

A particular type of support that appears to provide a buffer against burnout and TRES is provided by professionals' supervisors (Himle et al., 1989; Kim & Lambie, 2018). A lack of supervisor support and supervision decreases the ability to cope with employment stress (Barak et al., 2001) and is associated with professional burnout (Kim & Lambie, 2018; Newell & MacNeil, 2010).

This type of supervisory support includes structuring work expectations and directly acknowledging and addressing employment stressors (Taunton et al., 1997), such as the burden associated with working with traumatized clients. For example, social workers who perceive their supervisors as being supportive are less likely to experience professional burnout (Lloyd et al., 2002) and employment-related traumatic stress (Lynch, 2019). Professionals, who view themselves as being supported by supervisors, report less emotional exhaustion and depersonalization and a greater sense of personal accomplishment (Rupert et al., 2015). Particularly relevant to trauma-related employment stress is the observation that support offered by supervisors has been identified as crucial to the prevention of STS (Lynch, 2019). Supervisors of professionals working with traumatized clients who view STS as being the individual professional's challenge and do not provide guidance on the reality of STS, or how to manage it or provide resources needed to combat STS, will likely have high rates of professional turnover with their supervisees (Jirek, 2020).

Peers

In addition to support offered by supervisors, coworker support and environments that promote teamwork (vs. independent practice) buffer against burnout and employment-related traumatic stress (Um & Harrison, 1998). For example, Vilardaga et al. (2011) reported that the more support psychotherapists received from colleagues, the less emotional exhaustion and the more feelings of personal accomplishment reported. Conversely, a lack of support from professional colleagues is associated with burnout (Newell & MacNeil, 2010). In the words of Maslach and Leiter (2016):

> When these [work] relationships are characterized by a lack of support and trust, and by unresolved conflict, then there is a greater risk of burnout. On the contrary, when these job-related relationships are working well, there is a great deal of social support, employees have effective means of working out disagreements, and they are more likely to experience job engagement. (p. 105)

Organizational Responses to Burnout and TRES

While it would appear that burnout and TRES prevention programs are effective (Awa et al., 2010), study of such is limited. For example, a 2020 PsycINFO database search conducted using the search terms "burnout prevention," "compassion fatigue prevention," "secondary stress prevention," and "vicarious trauma prevention" yielded 383, 33, 22, and 5 documents, respectively. Further, an examination of these documents revealed very few that address the organization's role in the prevention of burnout and, in particular, TRES (Jirek, 2020). That said, from the available literature, as well as the organizational factors identified in the first part of this chapter, some recommendations can be offered. We do so by making use of O'Malley et al.'s (2017) framework for "organizational resilience," which suggest that to address trauma-related employment stress organizations should (a) address organizational culture and leadership, (b) focus on prevention, (c) promote early identification and intervention, and (d) critically evaluate organizational efforts to address the work-related injuries.

Organizational Culture and Leadership

O'Malley et al. (2017) suggest that an organizational response to burnout and employment-related traumatic stress begins by critically examining workplace norms and ensuring that they are trauma-informed. The organization needs to acknowledge the realities of these workplace injuries and view prevention as an ethical responsibility (and may even make staff self-care a part of their mission statement; Bell et al., 2003). Doing so would require the organization to ensure that the training and support their professionals need to do their jobs is offered, while at the same time minimizing the effects of these work-related injuries. Similarly, organizational leaders need to be well versed in burnout and employment-related traumatic stress and shape their supervision and work management in a fashion consistent with trauma-informed practices (Bell et al., 2003).

Organizational leaders need to minimize work not directly associated with direct client service and administrative and paperwork demands. Giving the professional some say in (or to the degree possible, control over) work assignments and the completion of these tasks may also serve to help protect them from these work-related injuries (Chen et al., 2019).

Professionals working within an organization need to view the work environment as fair and equitable. One approach to doing so, cited by Maslach et al. (2001), involved having weekly group staff meetings wherein organizational leaders and staff members discussed ways to reduce observed inequities. Relative to a control group, participants in these groups reported reduced emotional exhaustion and greater perceived equity.

Organizational leaders also need to attend to the physical work environment, which sets a tone and influences work culture. In addition to ensuring that professionals have the physical resources, they need to provide client services: the environment must be accessible, comfortable, safe, and secure for all racial/ethnic groups, genders, sexualities, etc. Recognizing that the workplace culture can perpetuate feelings of isolation and stress especially among marginalized groups, organizations should promote awareness about implicit bias (attitudes and/or preconceptions that influence behavior) and microaggression (an external expression of implicit bias). When people experience work places that diminish or dismiss employee stress, the environment may worsen chronic stress, reactivate emotional wounds, and contribute to re-traumatization of employees (O'Malley et al., 2017). Organizations must address discrimination-related stress or trauma and validate any perceived oppression.

Monitoring and managing workload is an obvious first step in the primary prevention of burnout and TRES. To minimize these work-related injuries, the organization needs to ensure that work weeks do not exceed 40 h, and ideally are under 35 h (Hu et al., 2016; Warren et al., 2013). In addition, careful attention should be given to caseloads, with particular care, attention, supervision, and support given to those assignments with a high ratio of traumatized and otherwise challenging clients. Ensuring that professionals have diverse caseloads (versus caseloads composed primarily with traumatized clients) has been associated with reductions in VT. Additionally, it is not unheard of for traumatized clients to display threatening behaviors. Thus, physical safety of all organizational employees must be considered (Bell et al., 2003).

In addition to these more basic forms of prevention, organizations must assertively promote self-care and an awareness of its importance in addressing burnout and TRES. Organizations should celebrate, not simply tolerate (let alone punish), employees who engage in the self-care needed to address these work-related injuries. Especially in settings where professionals work with a high percentage of traumatized clients, it will be important to destigmatize STS (O'Malley et al., 2017). Providing, or making available, direct instruction of the causes, consequences, and management of burnout and TRES is essential and has been found to be effective (Chen et al., 2019; Schoeps et al., 2019).

Training resources can include web-based tools and mobile applications (Pospos et al., 2018). The Compassion Fatigue Awareness Project's (http://compassionfatigue.org) mission statement includes the promotion of awareness and understanding of compassion fatigue and its effect on caregivers and might be one source for such training. In addition, Table 6.1 provides examples of such psychoeducational

Table 6.1 Psychoeducational resources for the prevention of burnout and trauma-related employment stress

Program	Description	Available
Compassion Fatigue 101	Explores the essentials of compassion fatigue	https://www.tendacademy.ca/product/compassion-fatigue-101-course/
Resilience Within Trauma-Exposed Environments	Provides a framework to understand stress mechanisms and resilience in trauma-exposed environments. Introduces approaches to increasing resilience and enhancing individual wellness and organizational health	https://www.tendacademy.ca/product/resilience-in-trauma-exposed-work-training/
Staying Grounded in Stressful Work	Provides skills to move professionals out of states of reactivity or avoidance and to be better able to choose how to respond.	https://www.tendacademy.ca/product/wtf-strategies-to-keep-helping-professionals-grounded-and-centered/
Support for Teachers Affected by Trauma (STAT)	Designed to increase understanding of STS and provides techniques and resources to mitigate its effects	https://statprogram.org/training

resources offered by the TEND Academy (https://www.tendacademy.ca) and Support for Teachers Affected by Trauma (STAT; https://statprogram.org/training) that are specifically oriented toward addressing (TRES).

Social support and empathetic supervision are other essential elements of organizational efforts to prevent burnout and TRES (Bell et al., 2003). The assertive promotion of connectedness and positive relationships with others (both supervisors and coworkers) in the work environment is essential. Engaging in team building activities and promotion of a favorable team environment that emphasizes collaboration should be an important target of prevention efforts (Bell et al., 2003; Chen et al., 2019; Hu et al., 2016; Reyes Ortega et al., 2019).

Training Programs

Weaving in self-care strategies and education about burnout and TRES into the curricula of training programs for the helping professions is recommended. Many organizations, including the American Nurses Association Code of Ethics for Nurses (Linton & Koonmen, 2020) and the National Association of School Psychologists (NASP, 2020), have added self-care for the practitioner into their ethical standards. Evidence of these standards in training programs is required for association accreditation in some cases (NASP, 2020). In their study of registered veterinarians, Hatch et al. (2011) concluded that modifying the curricula of veterinary schools to include self-care awareness and strategies, along with opportunity to enhance these skills throughout students' veterinary careers, could result in improved mental health, increased job engagement and work satisfaction, and decreased burnout. Therefore, it is recommended for most, if not all, helping professions that self-care should be taught, just as any other ethical or legal principle, starting within respective training programs.

Bibliotherapy

Bibliotherapy is the use of books or manuals (e.g., self-help books) to walk readers through the steps of a treatment (Carlbring et al., 2011). Bibliotherapy has proven effective in reducing psychological problems such as anxiety, depression, and obsessive-compulsive disorder symptoms (Moritz et al., 2019; Naylor et al., 2007; Ritzert et al., 2020). Use of books about ACT for personal use could be another viable intervention to reduce burnout and TRES in the work setting. In a study by Jeffcoat and Hayes (2012), ACT bibliotherapy was used as an intervention with K-12 school personnel. In pre-intervention, three-fourths of the participants were above clinical cutoffs in impaired general mental health, depression, anxiety, or stress. Participants who read the ACT book for two months, including completing the exercises and quizzes, showed significant improvement in psychological health, including reduced stress, anxiety, and depressive symptoms as compared with the wait-list control group. These findings lend support to the utility of self-study as an intervention.

A recommendation for organizations is to consider having a brief in-service on the topic of ACT, then provide a workbook, such as "ACT Made Simple" by Russ Harris (2009), or "Get Out of Your Mind and Into Your Life" by Hayes (2005), for individual practice at home. Weekly or monthly meetings could be scheduled wherein the content and activities are discussed as they apply to the participant's experiences.

Identification and Intervention

Encouraging self-screening and supporting the prompt identification of burnout and TRES should also be institutionalized (O'Malley et al., 2017). Maslach et al. (2019) and Stamm (2012) both offer empirically supported measures of these work-related injuries, with the latter having a version specifically for self-screening (https://proqol. org/uploads/ProQOL_5_English_Self-Score.pdf). In addition to self-screening, supervisors should be vigilant for the signs of burnout and TRES and, as indicated, make adjustments to work and caseloads. Hu et al. (2016) have suggested that it might be most effective to look for a better match between the individual and their assignments, rather than simply reducing work and caseloads. They offer that if professionals view their work as valuable, rewarding, and important, they may better tolerate work demands. Finally, depending on the severity of the injury, there may be the need for psychotherapeutic care and referrals to the organization's employee assistance program. To the extent the supervisor makes such care referrals, a "warm hand-off" is recommended. In other words, instead of simply directing the professional to contact a treatment provider, the supervisor should offer to help identify such providers and assist in making initial contact with them (O'Malley et al., 2017).

Ongoing Evaluation

Finally, O'Malley et al. (2017) recommend that the organization engage in ongoing evaluation of the effectiveness of prevention efforts and response to burnout and TRES. Being open to and seeking out feedback from all members of the organization is essential to ensuring that trauma-informed organizational practices are effective. All members of the organizational community must feel free to let supervisors know of factors that may contribute to burnout and TRES without fear of retribution.

Resources for Organizations

Adapted from a listing offered by O'Malley et al. (2017), Table 6.2 offers resources for organizations. These would be helpful for any agency looking to improve its trauma-informed practices.

Table 6.2 Trauma-informed practice resources for organizations

Program	Description	Available
Headington Institute	Partners with humanitarian relief and development organizations and emergency responders before, during, and after deployment to ensure well-being	https://headington-institute.org
National Child Traumatic Stress Network	Strives to increase the standard of care and improve access to services for traumatized children, their families, and communities	https://www.nctsn.org
	Secondary Traumatic Stress: A Fact Sheet for Organizations Employing Community Violence Workers	https://www.nctsn.org/resources/secondary-traumatic-stress-fact-sheet-organizations-employing-community-violence-workers
	Organizational Secondary Traumatic Stress: A webinar addresses the impact of STS in organizational settings	https://learn.nctsn.org/enrol/index.php?id=236
	Secondary Trauma and Child Welfare Staff: Guidance for Supervisors and Administrators	https://www.nctsn.org/resources/secondary-trauma-and-child-welfare-staff-guidance-supervisors-and-administrators
The Secondary Traumatic Stress Informed Organization Assessment Tool	Assessment tool used to evaluate the degree to which an organization is STS-informed, and able to respond to the impact of STS in the workplace	https://www.uky.edu/ctac/stsioa
TEND Academy	Offers resources and training for addressing work in high-stress workplaces where trauma exposure is common	https://www.tendacademy.ca/courses-2/
	Organizational Health in Trauma-Exposed Environments. An online course for managers and supervisors of teams working in high stress, trauma-exposed environments	https://www.tendacademy.ca/product/organizational-health-in-trauma-exposed-environments-essentials/
	Online Compassion Fatigue Educator Program. Participants gain the skills/tools needed to deliver workshops on compassion fatigue and secondary trauma within high-stress and trauma-exposed workplaces	https://www.tendacademy.ca/product/online-cfe-spring-2020/

Concluding Comments

Preventing and addressing burnout and TRES is not simply the responsibility of the individual professional. Organizations themselves need to institutionalize practices that support the mental wellness of their employees, minimize the chances of burnout and TRES, and have protocols and procedures in place for responding to employees who suffer from these health problems. Doing so makes sense from a number of different perspectives. Arguably, first and foremost keeping employees healthy is simply the right thing to do. But beyond this humanistic goal, attending to burnout and TRES will also better ensure that the core mission (or bottom line) of the organization is achieved. Healthy employees will better meet the needs of the organization's clients and in doing so better ensure organizational success.

References

Acker, G. M. (2010). The challenges in providing services to clients with mental illness: Managed care, burnout and somatic symptoms among social workers. *Community Mental Health Journal, 46*, 591–600. https://doi.org/10.1007/s10597-009-9269-5.

Aronsson, G., Theorell, T., Grape, T., Hammarström, A., Hogstedt, C., Marteinsdottir, I., Skoog, I., Träskman-Bendz, L., & Hall, C. (2017). A systematic review including meta-analysis of work environment and burnout symptoms. *BMC Public Health, 17*(264), 1–13. https://doi.org/10.1186/s12889-017-4153-7.

Awa, W. L., Plaumann, M., & Walter, U. (2010). Burnout prevention: A review of intervention programs. *Patient Education and Counseling, 78*(2), 184–190. https://doi.org/10.1016/j.pec.2009.04.008.

Barak, M. E. M., Nissly, J. A., & Levin, A. (2001). Antecedents to retention and turnover among child welfare, social work, and other human service employees: What can we learn from past research? A review and metanalysis. *Social Service Review, 75*(4), 625–661. http://www.jstor.com/stable/10.1086/32316.

Bell, H., Kulkarni, S., & Dalton, L. (2003). Organizational prevention of vicarious trauma. *Families in Society, 84*(4), 463–470. https://doi.org/10.1606/1044-3894.131.

Brock, S. E., Nickerson, A. B., Louvar Reeves, M. A., Conolly, C. N., Jimerson, S. R., Pesce, R. C., & Lazzaro, B. R. (2016). *School crisis prevention and intervention: The PREPaRE model* (2nd ed.). National Association of School Psychologists.

Carlbring, P., Maurin, T., Sjomark, J., Maurin, L., Westling, E., Ekselius, L., Cuijpers, P., & Andersson, G. (2011). All at once or one at a time? A randomized controlled trial comparing two ways to deliver bibliotherapy for panic disorder. *Cognitive Behavior Therapy, 40*(3), 228–235. https://doi.org/10.1080/16506073.2011.553629.

Chen, R., Austin, J. P., Sutton, J. P., Fussell, C., & Twiford, T. (2019). MFTs' burnout prevention and coping: What can clinicians, supervisors, training programs, and agencies do? *Journal of Family Psychotherapy, 30*(3), 204–220. https://doi.org/10.1080/08975353.2019.1655698.

Harris, R. (2009). *ACT made simple: A quick start guide to ACT basics and beyond.* New Harbinger.

Hatch, P., Winefield, H., Christie, B., & Lievaart, J. (2011). Workplace stress, mental health, and burnout of veterinarians in Australia. *Australian Veterinary Journal, 89*, 460–468. https://doi.org/10.1111/j.1751-0813.2011.00833.x.

Hayes, S. C. (2005). Get out of your mind and into your life: The new acceptance and commitment therapy. New Harbinger.

Hensel, J. M., Ruiz, C., Finney, C., & Dewa, C. S. (2015). Meta-analysis of risk factors for secondary traumatic stress in therapeutic work with trauma victims. *Journal of Traumatic Stress, 28*(2), 83–91. https://doi.org/10.1002/jts.21998.

Himle, D. P., Jayaratne, S., & Thyness, P. (1989). The effects of emotional support on burnout, work stress and mental health among Norwegian and American social workers. *Journal of Social Service Research, 13*(1), 27–45. https://doi.org/10.1300/J079v13n01_02.

Holman, L. F., Nelson, J., & Watts, R. (2019). Organizational variables contributing to school counselor burnout: An opportunity for leadership, advocacy, collaboration, and systemic change. *Professional Counselor, 9*(2), 126–141. https://eric.ed.gov/?id=EJ1221547.

Hu, N. C., Chen, J. D., & Cheng, T. J. (2016). The associations between long working hours, physical inactivity, and burnout. *Journal of Occupational and Environmental Medicine, 58*(5), 514–518. https://doi.org/10.1097/JOM.0000000000000715.

Jeffcoat, T., & Hayes, S. C. (2012). A randomized trial of ACT bibliotherapy on the mental health of K-12 teachers and staff. *Behaviour Research and Therapy, 50*(9), 571–579. https://doi.org/10.1016/j.brat.2012.05.008.

Jirek, S. L. (2020). Ineffective organizational responses to workers' secondary traumatic stress: A case study of the effects of an unhealthy organizational culture. *Human Service Organizations: Management, Leadership & Governance, 44*(3), 210–228. https://doi.org/10.1080/2330313 1.2020.1722302.

Kim, N., & Lambie, G. W. (2018). Burnout and implications for professional school counselors. *The Professional Counselor, 8*(3), 277–294. https://doi.org/10.15241/nk.8.3.277.

Lasalvia, A., Bonetto, C., Bertani, M., Bissoli, S., Cristofalo, D., Marrella, G., Ceccato, E., Cremonese, C., De Rossi, M., Lazzarotto, L., Marangon, V., Morandin, I., Zucchetto, M., Tansella, M., & Ruggeri, M. (2009). Influence of perceived organisational factors on job burnout: Survey of community mental health staff. *The British Journal of Psychiatry, 195*(6), 537–544. https://doi.org/10.1192/bjp.bp.108.060871.

Lee, R. T., & Ashforth, B. E. (1996). A meta-analytic examination of the correlates of the three dimensions of job burnout. *Journal of Applied Psychology, 81*(2), 123–133. https://doi.org/10.1037/0021-9010.81.2.123.

Lerias, D., & Byrne, M. K. (2003). Vicarious traumatization: Symptoms and predictors. *Stress and Health: Journal of the International Society for the Investigation of Stress, 19*(3), 129–138. https://doi.org/10.1002/smi.969.

Linton, M., & Koonmen, J. (2020). Self-care as an ethical obligation for nurses. *Nursing Ethics, 27*(8), 1694–1702. https://doi.org/10.1177/0969733020940371.

Lloyd, C., King, R., & Chenoweth, L. (2002). Social work, stress and burnout: A review. *Journal of Mental Health, 11*(3), 255–266. https://doi.org/10.1080/09638230020023642.

Lynch, R. J. (2019). Work environment factors impacting the report of secondary trauma in U.S. resident assistants. *Journal of College & University Student Housing, 46*(1), 62–78. https://digitalcommons.odu.edu/cgi/viewcontent.cgi?article=1061&context=efl_fac_pubs.

Maslach, C., & Leiter, M. P. (2016). Understanding the burnout experience: Recent research and its implications for psychiatry. *World Psychiatry, 15*(2), 103–111. https://doi.org/10.1002/wps.20311.

Maslach, C., Schaufeli, W. B., & Leiter, M. P. (2001). Job burnout. *Annual Review of Psychology, 52*, 397–422. https://doi.org/10.1146/annurev.psych.52.1.397.

Maslach, C., Jackson, S. E., Leiter, M. P., Schaufeli, W. B., & Schwab, R. L. (2019). *Maslach Burnout Inventory*. Mind Garden. https://www.mindgarden.com/117-maslach-burnout-inventory-mbi#horizontalTab4.

Moritz, S., Bernardini, J., & Lio, D. (2019). Effects and side effects of a transdiagnostic bias modification intervention in a mixed sample with obsessive-compulsive and/or depressive symptoms – a randomized controlled trial. *European Archives of Psychiatry and Clinical Neuroscience, 270*, 1025–1036. https://doi.org/10.1007/s00406-019-01080-3.

National Association of School Psychologists. (2020). *The professional standards of the National Association of School Psychologists.* https://www.nasponline.org/standards-and-certification/professional-ethics

Naylor, E. V., Antonuccio, D. O., Johnson, G., Spogen, D., & O'Donohue, W. (2007). A pilot study investigating behavioral prescriptions for depression. *Journal of Clinical Psychology in Medical Setting, 14*(2), 152–159. https://doi.org/10.10007/s10880-007-9064-9.

Newell, J. M., & MacNeil, G. A. (2010). Professional burnout, vicarious trauma, secondary traumatic stress, and compassion fatigue: A review of theoretical terms, risk factors, and preventive methods for clinicians and researchers. *Best Practices in Mental Health: An International Journal, 6*(2), 57–68. https://thedavidfollmergroup.com/best-practices-in-mental-health/.

O'Malley, M., Robinson, Y. A., Hydon, S., Caringi, J., & Hu, M. (2017). *Organizational resilience: Reducing the impact of secondary trauma on front line human services staff* (ReCAST issue brief). SAMHSA. http://files.constantcontact.com/bde05f96001/de8d7207-b6a8-440c-8e19-eea3dc5f5e1f.pdf?ver=1504885429000

Okoli, C. T. C., Seng, S., Otachi, J. K., Higgins, J. T., Lawrence, J., Lykins, A., & Bryant, E. (2019). A cross-sectional examination of factors associated with compassion satisfaction and compassion fatigue across healthcare workers in an academic medical Centre. *International Journal of Mental Health Nursing, 29*(3), 476–487. https://doi.org/10.1111/inm.12682.

Ozer, E. J., Best, S. R., Lipsey, T. L., & Weiss, D. S. (2003). Predictors of posttraumatic stress disorder and symptoms in adults: A meta-analysis. *Psychological Bulletin, 129*(1), 52–73. https://doi.org/10.1037/0033-2909.129.1.52.

Pospos, S., Young, I. T., Downs, N., Iglewicz, A., Depp, C., Chen, J. Y., Newton, I., Lee, K., Light, G. A., & Zisook, S. (2018). Web-based tools and mobile applications to mitigate burnout, depression, and suicidality among healthcare students and professionals: A systematic review. *Academic Psychiatry, 42*(1), 109–120. https://doi.org/10.1007/s40596-017-0868-0.

Reyes Ortega, M. A., Kuczynski, A. M., Kanter, J. W., Montis, I. A., & Santos, M. M. (2019). A preliminary test of a social connectedness burnout intervention for Mexican mental health professionals. *The Psychological Record, 69*(2), 267–276. https://doi.org/10.1007/s40732-019-00338-5.

Ritzert, T. R., Berghoff, C. R., Tifft, E. D., & Forsyth, J. P. (2020). Evaluating ACT processes in relation to outcome in self-help treatment for anxiety-related problems. *Behavior Modification, 44*(6), 865–890. https://doi.org/10.1177/0145445519855616.

Rupert, P. A., Miller, A. O., & Dorociak, K. E. (2015). Preventing burnout: What does the research tell us? *Professional Psychology: Research and Practice, 46*(3), 168–174. https://doi.org/10.1037/a0039297.

Schoeps, K., Tamarit, A., de la Barrera, U., & González Barrón, R. (2019). Effects of emotional skills training to prevent burnout syndrome in schoolteachers. *Ansiedad y Estrés, 25*(1), 7–13. https://doi.org/10.1016/j.anyes.2019.01.002.

Stamm, B. H. (2012). *Professional Qualify of Life: Compassion Satisfaction and Fatigue.* https://proqol.org/ProQol_Test.html

Taunton, R. L., Boyle, D. K., Woods, C. Q., Hansen, H. E., & Bott, M. J. (1997). Manager leadership and retention of hospital staff nurses. *Western Journal of Nursing Research, 19*(2), 205–226. https://doi.org/10.1177/019394599701900206.

Um, M. Y., & Harrison, D. F. (1998). Role stressors, burnout, mediators, and job satisfaction: A stress–strain–outcome model and an empirical test. *Social Work Research, 22*(2), 100–115. https://doi.org/10.1093/swr/22.2.100.

Vilardaga, R., Luoma, J. B., Hayes, S. C., Pistorello, J., Levin, M. E., Hildebrandt, M. J., Kohlenberg, B., Roget, N. A., & Bond, F. (2011). Burnout among the addiction counseling workforce: The differential roles of mindfulness and values- based processes and work-site factors. *Journal of Substance Abuse Treatment, 40*(4), 323–335. https://doi.org/10.1016/j.jsat.2010.11.015.

Vlăduţ, C. I., & Kállay, É. (2010). Work stress, personal life, and burnout: Causes, consequences, possible remedies—A theoretical review. *Cognition, Brain, Behavior: An Interdisciplinary*

Journal, 14(3), 261–280. https://www.scimagojr.com/journalsearch.php?q=21100860060&ti p=sid&clean=0.

Warren, C. S., Schafer, K. J., Crowley, M. E. J., & Olivardia, R. (2013). Demographic and work-related correlates of job burnout in professional eating disorder treatment providers. *Psychotherapy, 50*(4), 553–564. https://doi.org/10.1037/a0028783.

Yang, Y., & Hayes, J. A. (2020). Causes and consequences of burnout among mental health pro-fessionals: A practice-oriented review of recent empirical literature. *Psychotherapy, 57*(3), 426–436. https://doi.org/10.1037/pst0000317.

Chapter 7
Assessment, Resources, and Conclusion

This chapter provides both informal and formal assessment tools for well-being and current symptoms of burnout and TRES, along with helping resources. A summary of the book and our recommendations for future directions are also given.

Assessments for Burnout, TRES, and Wellness

Given the prevalence of these work-related challenges, we thought it would be productive to begin our examination of how individuals and systems can respond to the challenges of burnout and TRES with an informal self-assessment. By reflecting on the questions offered in Table 7.1, you might get a sense of the degree to which you are currently experiencing these challenges. For a more rigorous assessment of burnout using validated measures, consider making use of the additional tools also described in this chapter.

If you answered "yes" to questions 1–5, you are experiencing some of the symptoms of burnout. Answering "yes" to questions 6–10 would be consistent with CF, and "yes" to questions 11–15 would be consistent with STS (which is also often identified as VT).

Next we discuss burnout, TRES, and wellness measures with at least some established psychometric properties. Table 7.2 summarizes these measures, which are discussed in greater detail in this chapter.

M. L. Holland et al., *Burnout and Trauma Related Employment Stress*,
https://doi.org/10.1007/978-3-030-83492-0_7

Table 7.1 To what extent are you experiencing burnout or TRES

1. I feel exhausted much of the time.
2. I feel as if I have "run out of gas" when it comes to completing my work.
3. I do not feel as "connected" to my job or my profession as I once did.
4. I have negative feelings about my job and am increasingly cynical about the value of my work.
5. I am feeling less and less effective in my work.
6. I no longer find caring for others satisfying.
7. I have lost the desire to engage in continuing professional development.
8. I feel hopeless when it comes to helping my clients.
9. I no longer like being a caregiver.
10. I no longer feel like I am an effective caregiver.
11. I can't stop thinking about my client's traumatic circumstances.
12. I avoid discussion of my client's traumatic experiences.
13. I am increasingly agitated, irritable, and easily angered.
14. I am easily startled.
15. I find it difficult to concentrate even outside of work.

The Professional Quality of Life (ProQOL)

The *Professional Quality of Life* (ProQOL; Stamm, 2012) assessment is a tool measuring the positive and negative effects of helping people who are experiencing trauma and/or suffering. The *ProQOL* is widely validated and can provide insight about yourself and your environment by assessing the balance of your negative and positive work-related and personal experiences. While the measure does not provide diagnostic information, it does assess areas important for mental well-being including compassion satisfaction, compassion fatigue, and compassion stress. The results may help identify areas that may need increased self-care.

Maslach Burnout Inventory–Human Services Survey (MBI-HSS) for Medical Personnel

The *Maslach Burnout Inventory–Human Services Survey for Medical Personnel* (MBI-HSS MP; Maslach et al., 2019) is a 22-item instrument measuring three areas: depersonalization (DP), emotional exhaustion (EE), and low sense of personal accomplishment (PA). This measure has respondents answer questions by choosing among frequency rating choices ranging from "Never" to "Every day." The *MBI-HSS* is designed for adults working in helping professions or human service jobs (e.g., social workers, teachers, police officers, and nurses). The *MBI-HSS* has been translated into German (Aiken et al., 2001), Hebrew (Chayu & Kreitler, 2011), Chinese (Yao et al., 2013), Japanese (Poghosyan et al., 2010), and Turkish (Akkuş et al., 2010).

Table 7.2 Burnout, TRES, and wellness screening tools

Name	Brief description	Cost	Link
The Professional Quality of Life (ProQOL; Stamm, 2012)	Measures three critical areas important for mental wellbeing: Compassion satisfaction, compassion stress, and compassion fatigue	$0. Publicly available	https://proqol.org/ProQol_Test.html
Maslach Burnout Inventory – Human Services Survey for Medical Personnel (MBI-HSS MP; Maslach et al., 2019)	Measures burnout in individuals who work with other people (e.g., medical professionals and human services)	$15 for the individual report; $200 for the group report. Permission can be obtained from www.mindgarden.com	https://www.mindgarden.com/117-maslach-burnout-inventory-mbi
Oldenburg Burnout Inventory (Demerouti et al., 2003).	Measures burnout in any occupation	$0. Publicly available	https://www.papsych.org/uploads/1/0/3/6/10362808/oldenburg_burnout_inventory.pdf
Single Item Burnout Measure (Dolan et al., 2015)	Measures burnout in any occupation	$0. Publicly available	Access the Single Item Burnout Measure
Copenhagen Burnout Inventory (Kristensen et al., 2005)	Measures burnout in any occupation	$0. Publicly available	https://nfa.dk/da/Vaerktoejer/Sporgeskemaer/Sporgeskema-til-maaling-af-udbraendthed/Copenhagen-Burnout-Inventory-CBI
The Stanford Professional Fulfillment Index (PFI; Trockel et al., 2018)	Measures burnout and professional fulfillment, specifically in physicians	Publicly available (in article). There is no cost for nonprofit organizations using the survey for program evaluation and/or research. However, there is a cost for commercial use and/or for profit organizations	For more information contact the Stanford risk authority at wellness.surveyteam@TheRiskAuthority.com

(continued)

Table 7.2 (continued)

Name	Brief description	Cost	Link
Well-being index (Dyrbye et al., 2010)	Identifies various indicators of distress including burnout, low physical/mental quality of life, fatigue, anxiety/stress, and depression	The WBI is free for use in efforts to improve nonprofit organizations and for research use. An interactive version that provides individualized feedback is also free for individual use. There is an organizational version available for purchase. Contact for pricing: https://www. mywellbeingindex.org/commercial-pricing#estim ate=3/1/1000/2/	https://www.mededwebs.com/ well-being-index. Access the Well-Being Index

Oldenburg Burnout Inventory

The *Oldenburg Burnout Inventory* (Demerouti et al., 2003) can be utilized for adults working in any occupational group. The *Oldenburg Burnout Inventory* purports to measure burnout though 16 items covering two areas: work disengagement (negative attitudes toward work) and exhaustion (physical, affective, and cognitive aspects). The measure includes multiple questions and requires responses in the form of four-point Likert scale ratings from (1) "Strongly Agree" to (4) "Strongly Disagree."

Single Item Burnout Measure

The *Single Item Burnout Measure* (Dolan et al., 2015) assesses levels of burnout in any occupational group. Response options are:

> "I enjoy my work, I have no symptoms of burnout.
> Occasionally I am under stress and I don't always have as much energy as I once did, but I don't feel burned out.
> I am definitely burning out and have one or more symptoms of burnout, such as physical and emotional exhaustion.
> The symptoms of burnout that I am experiencing won't go away. I think about frustration at work a lot.
> I feel completely burned out and often wonder if I can go on. I am at a point where I may need some changes or may need to seek some sort of help." (p. 585).

An endorsement of the first two responses indicates no symptoms of burnout, whereas an endorsement of any of the other responses (3, 4, or 5) indicates symptoms of burnout.

Copenhagen Burnout Inventory

The *Copenhagen Burnout Inventory* (Kristensen et al., 2005) is a 19-item survey that can be used to measure burnout in adults from any occupational group. Responses are reported on a five-point scale ranging from "Always/Very High Degree" to "Never or Almost Never/Very Low Degree" and cover three areas: personal, work, and client-related burnout. Scores can range from 0 to100; higher scores on the survey indicate a higher degree of burnout. The *Copenhagen Burnout Inventory* is publicly available.

Stanford Professional Fulfillment Index

The *Stanford Professional Fulfillment Index* (PFI; Trockel et al., 2018) is a 16-item instrument measuring burnout (e.g., interpersonal disengagement and work exhaustion) and professional fulfillment in adults in a health care setting and physicians. Responses are reported on a five-point scale ranging from "Not at all true" to "Extremely." A higher score on the professional fulfillment scale is favorable, while higher scores on the work exhaustion or interpersonal disengagement scales are less favorable. The *PFI* is publicly available at no cost for nonprofit organizations (for research or program evaluation); however, there is a cost for commercial use or use by for-profit organizations.

Well-Being Index

The *Well-Being Index* (WBI; Dyrbye et al., 2010) is a tool used to identify various indicators of distress (e.g., burnout, depression, fatigue, anxiety/stress, and low quality of life) in adults in any occupational group. The *WBI* has a seven- or nine-item version with yes/no response categories and includes personalized feedback and links to resources. The individual measure is free to the public. The WBI also has an organizational version that provides feedback, links to resources, and reports but requires a fee for use.

Helping Resources

As we conclude this book, we bring to your attention resources suggested to further support the work of professionals and their employers in addressing the challenges of burnout and TRES and to promote mental wellness. By no means is this list comprehensive, but rather a start for how to begin to access other resources that may be able to support you. In this section, we briefly describe each resource and offer guidance on how they can be accessed.

American Psychological Association (APA)

On this webpage, the APA offers links to multiple questionnaires commonly used with adults and in caregiver research. The link to this page is: https://www.apa.org/pi/about/publications/caregivers/practice-settings/assessment/tools/mental-health-caregivers

Compassion Fatigue Awareness Project (CFAP)

The CFAP, associated with Healthy Caregiving LLC, offers training materials (e.g., "The Caregivers Bill of Rights, "The Ten Laws" [to creating a healthy workplace]), a "ProQoL Pocket Card," and links to several books from the project's founder (Patricia Smith). These resources can be accessed via: https://www.compassionfatigue.org

Mayo Clinic

Acknowledging the stress of being a caregiver, the Mayo Clinic offers a listing of stress management strategies. This webpage includes a variety of links designed to protect individuals for stress and to support overall mental well-being. This webpage can be accessed at: https://www.mayoclinic.org/healthy-lifestyle/stress-management/in-depth/caregiver-stress/art-20044784

Not One More Vet (NOMV)

NOMV is an online support network of over 26,000 veterinary professionals helping with topics such as compassion fatigue, depression, and suicide. It provides a variety of robust programs created to assist veterinary professionals through education, resources, and support. Their webpage can be located at: https://nomv.org/

TEDx: Quality of Life

Offered by Patricia Smith (the founder of CFAP), this TED Talk acknowledges that caregivers are often so busy caring for others they often ignore their own health. This video, which offers strategies for addressing compassion fatigue, can be accessed via: https://www.youtube.com/watch?v=7keppA8XRas&t=17s

The National Center on Family Homelessness (NCFH)

The NCFH offers assistance for the helper in assessing their current stress levels and implementing self-care via the workbook, "What about you? A workbook for those that work with others." Available at: http://508.center4si.com/SelfCareforCareGivers.pdf

The National Child Traumatic Stress Network (NCTSN)

The NCTSN has as its stated mission raising "the standard of care and improve access to services for traumatized children, the families and communities..." (https://www.nctsn.org). Consistent with the theme of this book, the NCTSN acknowledges the impact working with traumatized youth can have on professionals. Thus, in addition to further describing the cause and consequences of STS, specific resources developed by the NCTSN are offered. These resources can be accessed via: https://www.nctsn.org/trauma-informed-care/secondary-traumatic-stress

SUNY Buffalo, School of Social Work

The University of Buffalo offers tips and ideas for how to integrate self-care into your daily schedule. Information available at: http://socialwork.buffalo.edu/resources/self-care-starter-kit/developing-your-self-care-plan.htm

The Vicarious Trauma Toolkit: Blueprint for a Vicarious Trauma-Informed Organization

Consistent with Chap. 6's discussion of organizational responsibilities to address the challenges of TRES, the US Office for Victims of Crime offers this extensive toolkit designed to provide employers with the knowledge and skills needed to address the vicarious trauma of their professional staff members. This resource, which "focuses on the organizational response to work related trauma exposure," can be accessed via: https://ovc.ojp.gov/program/vtt/introduction

Summary and Future Directions

In the pages of this book, we hope to have provided the reader with strategies to address the challenges of working in a helping profession and the, at times, toxic effects of professional work with clients who have experienced, or are experiencing, traumatic stress. We hope to have armed the reader with a better understanding of burnout and TRES and specific strategies for addressing these employment-related health challenges. The focus of this book has primarily been on addressing the individual experiencing burnout and TRES, which we believe is consistent with the ethical mandate for professionals to deliberately engage in the self-care necessary to prevent these challenges. However, we do not mean this to imply that employers have no responsibility. Quite the opposite, we believe strongly that for organizational missions to be achieved, organizations themselves must attend to employee mental wellness. In fact, as we look toward the future of work and scholarship in this area, we hope to find more resources like The Vicarious Trauma Toolkit: Blueprint for a Vicarious Trauma-Informed Organization (cited in the Helping Resources section above) and an overall greater emphasis placed on the role of the organization in preventing and reducing burnout and TRES.

References

Aiken, L. H., Clarke, S. P., Sloane, D. M., & Sochalski, J. (2001). Cause for concern: Nurses' reports of hospital care in five countries. *LDI Issue Brief, 6*, 1–4. http://www.ncbi.nlm.nih.gov/pubmed/12524707.

Akkuş, Y., Karacan, Y., Göker, H., & Aksu, S. (2010). Determination of burnout levels of nurses working in stem cell transplantation units in Turkey. *Nursing & Health Sciences, 12*(4), 444–449. https://doi.org/10.1111/j.1442-2018.2010.00557.x.

Chayu, T., & Kreitler, S. (2011). Burnout in nephrology nurses in Israel. *Nephrology Nursing Journal, 38*(1), 65–77. http://www.ncbi.nlm.nih.gov/pubmed/21469556.

Demerouti, E., Bakker, A. B., Vardakou, I., & Kantas, A. (2003). The convergent validity of two burnout instruments. *European Journal of Psychological Assessment, 19*(1), 12–23. https://doi.org/10.1027/1015-5759.19.1.12.

Dolan, E. D., Mohr, D., Lempa, M., Joos, S., Fihn, S. D., Nelson, K. M., & Helfrich, C. D. (2015). Using a single item to measure burnout in primary care staff: A psychometric evaluation. *Journal of General Internal Medicine, 30*(5), 582–587. https://doi.org/10.1007/s11606-014-3112-6.

Dyrbye, L. N., Szydlo, D. W., Downing, S. M., Sloan, J. A., & Shanafelt, T. D. (2010). Development and preliminary psychometric properties of a well-being index for medical students. *BMC Medical Education, 10*(8), 1–9. https://doi.org/10.1186/1472-6920-10-8.

Kristensen, T. S., Borritz, M., Villadsen, E., & Christensen, K. B. (2005). The Copenhagen Burnout Inventory: A new tool for the assessment of burnout. *Work and Stress, 19*(3), 192–207. https://doi.org/10.1080/02678370500297720.

Maslach, C., Jackson, S. E., Leiter, M. P., Schaufeli, W. B., & Schwab, R. L. (2019). *Maslach Burnout Inventory.* Mind Garden. https://www.mindgarden.com/117-maslach-burnout-inventory-mbi#horizontalTab4

Poghosyan, L., Clarke, S. P., Finlayson, M., & Aiken, L. H. (2010). Nurse burnout and quality of care: Cross-national investigation in six countries. *Research in Nursing & Health, 33*(4), 288–298. https://doi.org/10.1002/nur.20383.

Stamm, B. H. (2012). *Professional Quality of Life: Compassion Satisfaction and Fatigue.* https://proqol.org/ProQol_Test.html

Trockel, M., Bohman, B., Lesure, E., Hamidi, M., Welle, D., Roberts, L., & Shanafelt, T. (2018). A brief instrument to assess both burnout and professional fulfillment in physicians: Reliability and validity, including correlation with self-reported medical errors, in a sample of resident and practicing physicians. *Academic Psychiatry, 42*(1), 11–24. https://doi.org/10.1007/s40596-017-0849-3.

Yao, Y., Yao, W., Wang, W., Li, H., & Lan, Y. (2013). Investigation of risk factors of psychological acceptance and burnout syndrome among nurses in China. *International Journal of Nursing Practice, 19*(5), 530–538. http://www.ncbi.nlm.nih.gov/pubmed/24093745.

Index

© The Author(s), under exclusive license to Springer Nature Switzerland AG 2022
M. L. Holland et al., *Burnout and Trauma Related Employment Stress*,
https://doi.org/10.1007/978-3-030-83492-0

Printed by Printforce, United Kingdom